1972   1973   1974   SPROUT/CAWLI.

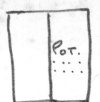

1975

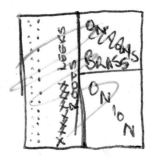

FRUIT and VEGETABLES

POTATOES .....
SPR. CAWLI CABBAGE   000
BEAN ✗ SWEET CORN ----
BEET CARROT. ECT.—.—

———

① POTATOES .
② BEANS LEEK
③ ROOTS
④ BRASSICAS.

Also available in the Pan Library of Gardening:
Roses and their cultivation
Garden Shrubs and Trees
Greenhouse and Indoor Plants

Pan Library of Gardening

FRUIT and VEGETABLES

Edited by Peter Hunt
Introduced by
Ray Procter, A.H.R.H.S.

 Pan Books Ltd: London

Published 1972 by
Pan Books Ltd.
33 Tothill Street, London SW1.

ISBN 0 330 02917 7

© Marshall Cavendish Ltd., 1969, 1972

Printed by Proost, Turnhout, Belgium.

The material contained in this book is
based on material first published in
'The Marshall Cavendish Encyclopedia of
Gardening', edited by Peter Hunt.

Contents

Glossary

Diploid A plant in which the number of chromosomes has neither increased nor decreased in the species during breeding or through other causes.

Friable The condition of the soil when it is easily workable.

Mulch A cover or topdressing spread over the surface of the soil.

Nymph The immature form of certain insects, e.g. the dragonfly, which resembles the adult (not to be confused with larvae or caterpillars, which do not resemble the adult).

Pollination The fertilisation with pollen.

Rootstock The root system upon which a cultivated variety of plant has been budded or grafted.

Variety A plant which is sufficiently different from others of its kind to be given a separate varietal name.

Vegetative propagation Propagation by methods other than by seed, e.g. by cuttings, layering, division, etc.

Introduction

by Ray Procter, A.H.R.H.S.

In the 1940s we grew more fruit and vegetables in our gardens than ever before. We had to. It was grim necessity. When the emergency passed and economic conditions improved, reaction set in and gratefully we returned to the cultivation of our flowers. That was only to be expected.

Today, however, there are sure signs that the pendulum is once again on the swing. There is a growing realisation of the rewards which follow the growing of fruit and vegetables in one's garden.

Some people might say that the growing of food rather than flowers satisfies some primaeval instinct. Perhaps this is purely a man's point of view: he is growing to provide for his family, whereas a woman prefers to grow flowers to adorn her home. Be that as it may, many of us find it deeply satisfying. We feel we are doing something truly useful and, however fascinating we may find the actual cultivation and however much fun we may get from it, our success can in the end be measured quantitively in the kitchen as well as qualitatively, by acclamation at your own table.

Enough of philosophising: there are good, sound, practical reasons for including both vegetables and fruit among the garden's occupants. With our feet firmly planted on the ground of our own garden, then, let us consider economic reasons. With prices rising as they recently have, and still are, any saving we can secure for our pocket is surely the most cogent of all reasons for raising vegetables and fruit.

Forget those Jeremiahs who point out that we can never grow cabbages as cheaply as the man who produces them by the acre. That is true, particularly if we take into account the hypothetical monetary value of our own time. But why should we? All garden work is fun and should be accounted as such. Expenditure on fertilisers and seeds, plants and trees, is soon balanced by the harvest, with shop prices as they are.

Remember that any saving you can achieve in the household expenditure leaves more in your pocket for something else. Every pound more to spend is equivalent to an increase in income of much more than that before the taxman claims his share.

In many families the garden is the source of luxuries—asparagus, baby marrows, early French beans, strawberries, peaches—which otherwise would be outside the scope of the household budget.

Cash saving, then, is one good practical reason for the home growing of fruit and vegetables. Next, I think, comes freshness which is closely bound with flavour.

After all, we eat for the sake of nourishment and the maximum nourishment is to be obtained from fruit and vegetables which have ripened naturally on the plant or in the ground and are consumed quickly before those elusive vitamins have vanished. Green vegetables, for instance, start to lose vitamin C the moment they are cut. It is probably no coincidence that really fresh fruit and vegetables taste better too.

Most young people today do not know what a green pea, fresh picked from the garden, tastes like. They know only the frozen, the canned or the dried, and we cannot describe to them what they are missing. By growing a row of peas in the garden we can give our family a new experience and perhaps recall once again one of the joys of our own childhood.

Peas are not singular in this respect. A tomato reddened only since picking can never taste the same as one ripened on the plant. New potatoes, dug from the garden and cooked immediately, are incomparable. So, too, with sweet corn—cut, cooked and eaten within the hour, it bears little resemblance to the greengrocer's cobs. Peaches and plums, picked when 'dead' ripe, warm in the sun—are they the same fruits as those hard, half-ripe or 'squishy' Victorias or peaches from some far-off Continental orchard which are all the local fruiterer can offer you?

So one could go on but every home gardener who takes up vegetable and fruit growing will soon begin to discover further examples of the magic of freshness and flavour to add to the list.

So far I have referred only to every day vegetables and fruits, the things we can grow at home and compare favourably with those in the shops. But what of the things one never sees in the shops?

Ask your greengrocer for Hamburg parsley, a pound of okra, some asparagus peas or a pe-tsai to go with your chop suey and see what sort of a look he will give you.

Here is another delight to be derived from home growing. You can enjoy all those unusual vegetables—and many more—and thus bring new flavours to the rather limited range to be found at most tables.

With fruit the advantage of home growing lies in choice of variety rather than in uncommon sorts of fruit. We can grow strawberries which really taste of strawberries, we can grow gage plums with their own rich special flavour so superior to that of ordinary plums. We do not have to worry about how well our crops will travel. We need not give first priority to yield—we can select varieties because

their flavour and sweetness and juiciness will more than compensate.

One word of warning : they say that it is the bad workman who blames his tools. More truly one notes that the good craftsman always has sound ones. Rather the same thing applies to the successful grower of vegetables and fruit—he begins with good seed and healthy stock. There are many so-called bargains on offer which prove the most expensive in the end. Patronise firms with a high reputation at stake : buy the best seed and, where this applies, fruit trees propagated from virus-tested stock, soft fruits from growers with Government inspection certificates.

No garden is too small for fruit and vegetables—you can grow strawberries in a window-box, herbs on the kitchen window sill—so why not start today?

Fruit trees and bushes

It is generally the aim of most amateur gardeners to grow fruit of some kind. The choice will depend on individual preference. Rarely, however, is it possible to find in one garden the fundamental conditions which will suit all fruits. The final choice may have to be made from those which experience and observation show to grow and crop best. It is not always understood or known that varieties of fruits differ in their suitability. Within the same area of a village or parish it is possible to have plants of the same variety of a fruit poles apart in growth and cropping.

Soils and situations Ideally the soil should be a deep and well-drained loam that has grown good vegetable crops for some years and so has a reserve of plant food. Shelter from wind will prevent most of the damage to the plants which, as a result, should grow stronger and better. The possibility of damage from frost cannot be overlooked so a gentle slope helps the cold heavier air to drain away and not persist over the plants. All plants do best in a position in full sun; shade from trees, hedges or buildings may result in poor growth.

The first feature to look for is the depth of the soil—the amount of usable ground overlying the parent material or rock underneath. Soils are generally deeper in valleys than on slopes or hill tops. Even on flat land the depth varies quite considerably. Man himself has also taken a hand by moving quite large amounts of soil for his own purposes.

Often the under soil or subsoil is pulled up and exposed to light and air for the first time. Such a soil will need careful handling and feeding to give even moderate results. Clay soils which are wet and sticky in winter but dry hard in summer can, if drained and well supplied with organic matter, give good yields. The use of mulches in summer in the area of the fruit plants will help winter drainage and keep them reasonably moist in a dry summer.

At the other extreme are gravel soils and those which contain much coarse sand. These are usually so poor that in summer they are very dry and fruit plants will flag for lack of water when they need it most.

In wet winters they are rarely water-logged and artificial drainage is unnecessary. Plenty of organic matter put into these soils will help in summer, aided by mulches in spring and summer to stop loss through evaporation. These and chalk soils are hungry for plant foods. Water should be handy for use in summer when rainfall is seldom enough for plant needs.

Soils with a high organic peat content can be most difficult for fruit plants except strawberries. They hold a great deal of water in most winters, but if there is a succession of dry years plants will look distressed—and peat needs a lot of water to rewet it.

Depth of true soil is as important as type of soil. All fruit plants can make more roots for anchorage and feeding than we imagine. The deeper the soil the better the plants will thrive. This does not mean they will make lush growth and crop indifferently.

When soil depth is less than 18 inches care will be needed as the plants become established; additional feeding and watering will be necessary. Strawberries, though deep rooting, are seldom in the same piece of ground for more than three years and sometimes less. For these soils 12–18 inches deep should be satisfactory. There are, of course, various ways of deepening some soils. The subsoil can be broken up by cultivation but left in its proper place, underneath the topsoil. In this way, total depth is increased and plant foods added to the surface and water are stored there while air, essential for good growth, gets in.

Preparation of the ground before planting should not be hurried. Plants will suffer and die very quickly if planted in freshly cultivated ground which may also be cold and wet. Soil which has grown a good crop of vegetables can be in excellent physical condition for fruit. If organic manures and fertilisers have been added generously for the vegetables, sufficient food is available to keep the plants growing nicely for a year or two. Where strawberries are concerned no more feeding may be needed or desirable. It should not be necessary to cultivate the ground after the vegetable crops, other than to remove weeds and plant debris. At this pre-planting stage the physical condition of the soil and its adequate depth are of first importance; feeding and water can be seen to later. The month of September should be the dead-line for soil preparation.

When the trees are to be planted in an existing grass area, part of this should be dug over early to allow the soil to settle.

Feeding Water is the first essential of

When ground is to be used for fruit cultivation, thorough preparation of the soil is important. Compost or other humus material is added to enrich the soil.

plant feeding. Without an adequate supply, growth and cropping will suffer. The period of greatest need is in the spring and summer. A deep soil will cope in most seasons but a shallow soil will not, and watering will have to be done. Newly planted trees or bushes will, in most seasons, need extra help and some form of mulching after watering will cut down loss by evaporation. The most critical months are April and May. Buds are bursting, flowers are opening, fruits forming and leaves expanding and shoots growing strongly, all making maximum demands for water.

One good watering in early May at 4 gallons per square yard, supplemented by a mulch of organic matter should see most fruit plants through the season.

If the rainfall in summer is very low, a further watering in June should suffice. Scrape away any previous mulch before watering and afterwards renew it.

Water alone will not keep plants healthy and profitable. Many elements (or chemicals) usually present in most soils are needed and of these nitrogen is the most important. Others needed in varying amounts are potash, phosphorus, iron, calcium, manganese and magnesium. Sometimes very small amounts of other trace elements such as boron are needed.

Although most fruit plants do best in slightly acid soils they do not thrive on those that are very acid. Calcium in the form of lime will help to preserve a balance. Where the soil is neutral or slightly acid, no lime need be added. If it is really acid, give a dressing of hydrated lime at 8 oz per square yard for 1–2 years and then have a soil test which should indicate what treatment is needed.

Organic matter in its many forms; farmyard manure, compost, shoddy, spent hops, peat, are all good in their own way but are not complete foods. Added to the soil, or used as mulches, they increase the general fertility and improve soil condition. They should, however, be supplemented if necessary. A wide range of artificial fertiliser

An adjustable 'Rainbow' plastic tree tie nailed in position on the stake.

mixtures is available and these can be very good if used sensibly.

It is possible to have a soil analysis made by the local county horticultural staff who, on the basis of the results, will give more detailed help, especially after examining the trees and bushes.

Cultivation Most fruit plants should be grown on clean, cultivated ground. It is, however, possible and sometimes necessary to grow grass round established trees. This makes it easier and more pleasant to get among the trees at all times of the year and provided the grass is cut often in summer no real harm should come to them. But in a dry season the grass, however short, will compete for food and water and this will have to be made good or the plants will suffer. Soft fruits grow best in cultivated ground and even here, competition from weeds can be considerable.

The ground around young fruit trees should be clear cultivated until they are well established. Modern weedkillers have eased the job of keeping ground clean.

After the plants have been put in the ground, the amount of cultivation done afterwards should, if possible, be restricted to the surface only. Deep cultivation close to the trees and bushes will certainly damage roots and restrict their feeding capacity. This may be all right if they are too vigorous, when this form of root pruning is useful.

If, after picking the fruit, deeper than surface cultivation has to be done to break up the hard surface and get rid of weeds, November is the best time to do it. The soil has a chance to settle and recover before the following spring. From March onwards only the top inch of the soil should be disturbed to keep weed seedlings from growing. The cultivated area acts as a mulch and cuts down evaporation of water; deeper cultivation does the opposite. Should any special soil treatment be necessary the effect is usually quickest on cultivated ground.

Where grass is grown round the trees this should not be allowed to grow more than 3–4 inches high during the summer

and the clippings should be left on the surface to rot.

It may be necessary to cut twelve or more times from March to September, depending on the rainfall. On light shallow soils a grass sward may make matters worse by starving the fruit plants of water unless extensive mulching is done with irrigation. On steeply sloping land grass will help to keep the soil in position and make management easier. When grass and weeds are growing round basically healthy but

neglected fruit trees, one of the first jobs is to get rid of the herbage and cultivate the surface. Don't cultivate deeply as most of the feeding roots are near the surface and are easily damaged. The trees should then respond to feeding treatment and after a year or two the area can go down to grass again.

In recent years chemical weedkillers have come to play a useful part in controlling a wide range of weeds and certain grass can be a real nuisance among fruit plants. Weeds not only smother plants but rob them of food and water. Before planting is done clear the ground of obvious weeds especially perennials—docks, thistles, bindweed and couch grass.

Choice of Plants Soil is rightly the basis of success in growing fruit, but choice of plants follows very closely. No one would choose poor, stunted, misshapen plants with unhealthy foliage. It is wise to take advantage of the disease-free fruit plants which nurserymen, helped by scientists, have produced.

In addition to improving the choice of all varieties of fruit, research workers have also given attention to the possibilities of growing smaller trees of apples, pears, plums and cherries. These could be more easily treated and harvested and would be ideal for the small garden.

Rootstocks A tree growing on its own roots is usually very uncertain in growth

Nylon string ties a tree firmly to the stake. Sacking prevents chafing.

and cropping and not adaptable for soils. For these reasons it is unwise, in most instances, to grow trees on their own roots. Because of this, rootstocks have been developed for many years. These are selected seedlings which are propagated vegetatively and from the root system and part, often small, of the main stem. They have great influence on the size of the tree of a particular variety as well as cropping, and the gardener has control over many of the habits of a variety on a selected rootstock. Some rootstocks make dwarf trees, others intermediate and some large. Scientists have concentrated their attention on dwarfing stocks as trees on these are much more manageable.

Apples have received most attention and for years the rootstock known as M.IX (and recently M.IX A) has been the standard dwarfing stock while M.II is still popular to make a large bush tree. Shortly after the Second World War a new selection of apple stocks was raised. This was largely a joint venture of East Malling Research Station and John Innes Horticultural Institute, at that time based at Merton. These rootstocks are known as MM (Malling-Merton selection). Some were picked for further trial and of these M.26 now shows great promise as a semi-dwarfing stock— slightly stronger than M.IX. Others are MM.104, MM.106, and MM.111, all of which make bigger bushes than MM.26 and are better yielding than M.II. If a very large tree is required M.24 is the

1 When watering soft fruit, a shallow basin is made with a hoe.
2 The basin is filled with water.
3 The soil is returned to the basin, then covered with a straw mulch.

best choice.

Quinces are used as the rootstock for pears. Most varieties today are grafted or budded on Quince A which makes a medium sized bush tree. A dwarfing Quince C was not successful but there are possibilities that this will be remedied soon.

There is no really dwarfing stock for plums though a selected common plum is worth trying. For a medium-sized tree use St. Julian. A dwarfing stock for sweet cherries still eludes the scientists

1, 2 and 3 When planting a fruit tree, spread the roots, plant to the old soil level and firm the soil around the roots. 4, 5 and 6 Two cross stakes are tied to the tree. A piece of sacking prevents rubbing.

but there is no doubt that the efforts to develop one will eventually be successful. The large tree which a sweet cherry makes is not suitable for the normal small garden.

Selection of Varieties Choice of varieties is very much a personal matter, but guidance must be sought from many sources—catalogues, books, experienced friends or neighbours and horticultural shows. The selection today, though not as great as in past years, is quite wide enough. Some old faithfuls have disappeared, but new names have taken their places. For economic reasons the nurseryman grows only those varieties which are in popular demand, mainly by the commercial grower.

In the garden there is, however, the opportunity to have a greater selection than in the orchard or plantation.

Dwarfing rootstocks and trained trees with more than one variety on each give scope for a fair selection—even out of the ordinary.

While there are advantages in having a very few varieties of particular fruits in the garden, there is evidence that there can be better and more regular yields if there is a fair selection, especially of tree fruits. Some varieties are known to yield good crops as lone trees. These are self-fertile or self-compatible and flowers on the plants will set fruits with their own pollen. Others will not and need the help of pollen from other varieties of the same kind of fruit.

Scientific investigation of many varieties has confirmed the findings of many gardeners and fruit growers that to grow one variety only is unwise. By following certain fertility rules, much disappointment can be avoided. The following tables should be used as a guide, in conjunction with personal taste and preference.

In general fruit plants can be divided into three groups:

(a) Self-compatible varieties are those which will set a full crop with their own pollen.

(b) Partially self-compatible varieties do not set a full crop with their own pollen.

(c) Self-incompatible varieties fail to set a crop with their own pollen.

Peaches will set better if the flowers are hand pollinated. Insects are few early in the year when the peach blooms.

Ideally, only self-compatible varieties would be planted, but since there are those not so favoured which have otherwise excellent qualities, some provision should be made to include them.

The self-compatible varieties are in this case, planted as pollinators. With the help of many insects, especially honey bees, pollen is transferred from variety to variety when the fruit plants are in full flower. This is termed cross-pollination. Provided the plants are fairly near to each other and the weather is favourable to insect movement all should be well. During cold, dull wet weather results may be less good, and even self-compatible varieties may not crop too well. Cross-pollination is bene-

1

ficial to the cropping of all varieties.

When selecting varieties for pollination choose those which are known to flower about the same time. With certain fruit plants—plums and cherries—even this is not good enough. To help with the selection reference should be made to the specially prepared tables below for further information.

Whichever variety is chosen as a pollinator it should be regular in flowering each year and overlap the flowering periods of other varieties by several days.

Apples Some varieties set no fruit at all when self pollinated, while others under favourable conditions set a fair crop. Yields are better when there are enough varieties for cross-pollination. There are a number of popular varieties which are poor pollinators (triploid varieties) but most are diploid, which pollinate each other very well. It is important to have at least two diploid varieties in a collection, unless the pollinator chosen is sufficiently self-fertile alone. When choosing varieties select those which will flower about the same time or overlap by a few days with others. There is some variation in the flowering periods of varieties but on the whole the times are very consistent. Winter temperatures and district can affect flowering periods.

In the following tables varieties are in seven flowering groups. Select if possible varieties within the same group

1 Apple 'Granny Smith' a firm green eating apple.
2 Apple 'Charles Ross' a good cropper, resistant to scab disease.

for pollination. The old very late variety 'Crawley Beauty' is sufficiently self-fertile to set a crop.

Cultivation Apples prefer deep loams but can be grown on sandy soils and heavy clays, if care is taken to drain wet soils and irrigate dry ones.

Cordons (planted 2½ feet by 6 feet), espaliers (10–18 feet apart), and arcure trained trees (3 feet by 6 feet), are grown against walls, fences or on post and wire

1 Apple 'Jonathan' a late rosy dessert apple.
2 Apple 'Cox's Orange Pippin' is a mid-season flowering variety.

supports; dwarf pyramids (3½ feet by 7 feet), spindle bushes (6 feet by 13 feet), pillars (5–6 feet by 10 feet), bush (12 feet by 12 feet), and half-standards (15–18 feet by 15–18 feet), on an open, but sheltered, site. Provide wind-breaks if natural shelter is not present.

Plant in November, if possible, or up to the end of March whenever the soil is sufficiently friable. It is best not to incorporate farmyard manure before planting into any except the poorest of soils. Plant as firmly as possible, ramming the soil round the roots with the square end of a stout post, and tie the tree to a substantial stake.

Flowering times for apples

Very early
Aromatic Russet (B)
Gravenstein (T)
Keswick Codlin (B)

Early
Adam's Pearmain (B)
Beauty of Bath
Bismark (B)
Cheddar Cross
Christmas Pearmain (B)
Discovery
Egremont Russet
George Cave
George Neal
Golden Spire
Irish Peach
Laxton's Early Crimson
Lord Lambourne
Lord Suffield
McIntosh Red
Melba (B)
Michaelmas Red
Norfolk Beauty
Patricia (B)
Rev W. Wilkes (B)
Ribston Pippin (T)
St Edmund's Pippin
Scarlet Pimpernal
Striped Beefing
Warner's King (T)
Washington (T)
White Transparent

Early mid season
Arthur Turner
Belle de Boskoop (T)
Blenheim Orange (TB)
Bowden's Seedling

Early mid season cont.
Bramley's Seedling (T)
Brownlee's Russet
Charles Ross
Claygate Pearmain
Cox's Orange Pippin
D'Arcy Spice
Devonshire Quarrenden (B)
Early Victoria (Emneth Early) (B)
Emperor Alexander
Epicure
Exeter Cross
Fortune (B)
Granny Smith
Grenadier
Howgate Wonder
James Grieve
John Standish
Jonathan
King's Acre Pippin
Kidd's Orange Red
Lord Grosvenor
Merton Pippin
Merton Prolific
Merton Russet
Merton Worcester
Miller's Seedling (B)
Ontario
Peasgood's Nonsuch
Red Victoria (B)
Reinette du Canada (T)
Rival (B)
Rosemary Russet
Sturmer Pippin
Sunset
Tydeman's Early Worcester
Tydeman's Late Orange
Wagener (B)
Winter Quarrenden (B)
Worcester Pearmain

Mid season
Allington Pippin (B)
Annie Elizabeth
Chelmsford Wonder (B)
Cox's Pomona
Delicious
Duke of Devonshire
Ellison's Orange
Golden Delicious
Golden Noble
Herring's Pippin
Lady Henniker
Lady Sudeley
Lane's Prince Albert
Laxton's Superb (B)
Monarch (B)
Orleans Reinette
Sir John Thornycroft

Late mid season
American Mother
Coronation (B)
Gascoyne's Scarlet
King of the Pippins (B)
Lord Derby
Merton Beauty
Newton Wonder
Northern Spy (B)
Royal Jubilee
William Crump
Winston
Woolbrook Pippin (B)

Late
Court Pendu Plat
Edward VII
Heusgen's Golden Reinette

Very late
Crawley Beauty

B=biennial or irregular flowering varieties. T=triploid varieties with poor pollen. Those not marked T are diploid varieties. Coloured sports eg Red Millar's Seedling usually flower at the same time as the parent.

2

3

Pears Varieties of pears are less fertile than apples. Even the variety 'Conference' is not self-fertile though trees will in poor pollination years produce parthenocarpic, i.e. seedless, fruits. A few varieties have sterile pollen and are quite useless as pollinators. Most varieties are diploid and may be used as pollinators for each other and for triploid varieties. There are, however, two groups of diploids which will neither set fruit with their own pollen nor pollinate

3 Pear 'Beurré Clairgeau' flowers early and is a golden skinned variety.

19

any variety in the same group. Group 1; Fondante d'Automne, Louise Bonne of Jersey, Précoce de Trevoux, Seckle and Williams' Bon Chrétien. Group 2; Beurré d'Amanlis and Conference.

For quality fruit the following planting distances should be regarded as the minimum: cordons (3 by 6 feet), fan-trained and espalier on 'Quince C' (12 feet apart), on 'Quince A' (15 feet apart), dwarf pyramids (4 by 7 feet), bush on 'Quince C' (12 feet each way), on 'Quince A' (15 feet each way), standard and half-standard (35 feet each way).

Flowering of pears

Early	Mid season	Late
Beurré Anjou	Belle-Julie	Beurré Bedford (MS)
Beurré Clairgeau	Beurré d'Amanlis	
Beurré Diel (T)	Beurré Six	Beurré Bosc
Comtesse de Paris	Beurré Superfin Conference	Beurré Hardy Bristol Cross (MS)
Doyenné d'Eté	Dr Jules Guyot	Catillac (T)
Duchesse d'Angoulême	Duchesse de Bordeaux	Clapp's Favourite
Easter Beurré	Durondeau	Doyenné du Comice
Emile d'Heyst	Fertility	
Louise Bonne of Jersey	Fondante d'Automne	Glou Morceau Gorham
Marguerite Marillat (MS)	Jargonelle Joséphine de	Hessle Laxton's Victor
Passe Crasanne	Malines	Marie Louise
Précoce de Trévoux	Merton Pride Packham's	Nouveau Poiteau Pitmaston
Princess	Triumph	Duchess (T)
Seckle	Souvenir du Congrès	Santa Claus
Uvedale's St Germain (T)	Thompson's Triomphe de	Winter Nelis
Vicar of Winkfield	Vienne	
Winter Orange	Williams' Bon Chrétien	

T = Triploid   MS = Male Sterile

Pear 'Packham's Triumph' is mid-season flowering. The tree is small but crops early, with yellow juicy fruit.

Plums While there are a number of plum varieties which will set fruit with their own pollen; there are others which will not. It is wise to make sure of pollination in a collection, by planting at least one known self-fertile variety.

In the following table varieties in group A will not set crops with their own pollen and those in group B will set poor crops only. In group C the varieties are self-compatible and should set good crops on their own but should not be relied on to do so. Many of the disappointments in the cropping of plums and gages stems from lack of adequate cross-pollination between varieties. In the following table suitable pollinators in each flowering period are marked * in group C.

No really satisfactory dwarfing root-stock has yet been found for plums. The two least vigorous are common plum and St Julien 'A'; the former, however, is only compatible with certain varieties. Trees grown on these rootstocks are sometimes described as 'semi-dwarf' but, even so, a standard or half-standard would be too large for the average garden, and even a bush-type tree requires a spacing of 12–15 feet (on Brompton or Myrobalan 'B' rootstock, 18–20 feet).

Because plums do not produce fruiting spurs as apples and pears do, they are not so amenable to training, and are seldom satisfactory as cordons or espaliers. They may, however, be grown as fans, for wall-training or with the support of posts and horizontal wires, but root-pruning will probably be necessary every five years or so to restrain growth and maintain fruiting (see Root

1 Plum 'Giant Prune' is a large oval fruit, cropping in mid-September.
2 Sweet Cherries are a little more difficult to grow than Morello Cherries which are usually wall-trained.

pruning). A fan tree on St Julien 'A' rootstock should be allotted at least 15 feet of wall space.

Plums may also be grown as semi-dwarf pyramids on St Julien 'A' rootstock and this is a form which is best for the small garden. Such a tree requires a spacing of 10 feet and, as it will never be allowed to grow much over 9 feet in height, it is possible to arrange some kind of cage or netting over the top of the tree to keep off birds, which will otherwise damage the fruit.

Flowering of plums

Compatibility Group A	Group B	Group C
Early		
Black Prince	Utility	Golden Transparent*
Jefferson		
Early mid season		
Black Diamond	Farleigh	Denniston's Superb
Coe's Golden	Damson	Monarch*
Drop		Ontario*
Late Orleans		Warwickshire
President		Drooper*
Mid season		
Bryanston Gage	Early Laxton	Bountiful
Kirke's Late	River's	Brandy Gage
Orange	Early	Czar*
Washington	Prolific	Laxton's Cropper
	Goldfinch	Laxton's Gage
		Merryweather Damson*
		Pershore
		Purple Pershore
		Severn Cross
		Victoria*
Late mid season		
Count Althann's	Cambridge	Blaisdon Red*
Gage	Gage	Early Transparent
Delicious	Early	Giant Prune
Pond's Seedling	Orleans	Oullins' Golden
Wyedale		Gage
Late season		
Late Transparent		Belle de Louvain*
Old Greengage		Belle de Septembre
Red Magnum Bonum		Marjorie's Seedling*
		Shropshire Damson

Flowering of Sweet Cherries   *Horizontal lines contain incompatibility groups*

Early	Early Mid season	Mid season	Late Mid season	Late	Very late
Early Rivers (E)	Bedford Prolific (EM) Circassian (EM) Knight's Early Black (EM)	Roundel (M) Circassian (EM) Knight's Early Black (EM)	Ronald's Heart (LM)		
Windsor (LM)	Bigarreau de Schrecken (EM) Waterloo (M) Merton Favourite (EM)	Frogmore Early (EM) Merton Bigarreau (EM) Merton Bounty (M)	Belle Agathe (VL)	Victoria Black A. (M) Black Elton (M)	
	Bigarreau de Mezel (M)		Emperor Francis (LM) Napoleon Bigarreau (LM) Ohio Beauty (L)		
Werder's Early Black (E)		Merton Premier (M)	Kent Bigarreau (LM)	West Midlands Bigarreau (M)	
	Turkey Heart (L)			Late Black Bigarreau (LM)	
	Merton Heart (EM)	Early Amber (EM) Governor Wood (EM) Elton Heart (M)			
		Bigarreau de Mezel (M)		Hooker's Black (M)	Bradbourne Black (LM) Géante d' Hedelfingen (LM)
		Peggy Rivers (EM)			
Red Turk (LM)					
Ramon Oliva (E)	Bigarreau Jaboulay (E)				
Guigne d'Annonay (VE)					
				Noble (L) Caroon (M)	

Universal donors   (will pollinate all varieties)

Early	Early Mid season	Mid season	Late Mid season	Late	Very late
Noir de Guben (LM) Goodnestone Black (EM) Nutberry Black (EM)	Mumford's Black (E) Tartarian E. (M)	Black Oliver (EM) Merton Glory (EM)	Smoky Dun (M)	Bigarreau Gaucher (L) Florence (L)	

Season of ripening: VE very early, E early, EM early mid season, M mid season, LM late mid season, L late, VL very late

Cherries Sweet cherry varieties will not set fruit with their own pollen and cross pollination will only achieve worthwhile crops if careful selection is made. Varieties in the same incompatibility group will not help each other to set fruit. They will crop only if pollinated by varieties in other groups, provided they are in the same flowering group.

Though some varieties of sour (acid) and Duke cherries are self-fertile, a number are not, but the problem of cross-pollination is simple. These varieties will also pollinate sweet cherries, but the reverse is not the case. In the table, left, the varieties are arranged in incompatibility groups.

Any variety in one of the following groups, flowers close enough to the others in a different group following or proceeding e.g. pollination for Frogmore could be Roundel (3), Circassian (2), or Napoleon (4) but not Waterloo (2) as this is in the same incompatibility group.

Sour cherries fruit on shoots formed the previous season. After the basic fan of branches has been built up by shortening the leaders annually as for sweet cherries, annually replaced sidegrowths are tied in parallel to the permanent branches. The replacement shoots are selected during May to August—one near the base of a fruiting shoot and another at its tip to draw sap to the fruit; all others are pinched out when quite small. The tip of the terminal shoot itself is pinched out when 3–4 inches of growth has been made.

After the cherries have been gathered, the fruited shoots are pruned back at their junction with the selected replacement shoots. The latter are then tied in neatly as before.

Peaches Most varieties are self-compatible, the principal exception is J. H. Hale which is male sterile, i.e. it has no good pollen. In view of the early flowering of most varieties when weather conditions are often poor, more than one variety should be planted.

Peaches are generally self-compatible, but it is advisable to plant more than one variety to ensure pollination.
1 Peach 'Peregrine', a variety with large fruits in mid-August.
2 Peach 'Stark Earliglo', with round yellow fruits.

Plant one to three-year-old trees between mid-October and mid-March, preferably in October or November. Trim any damaged roots, cover them with no more than 4–6 inches of soil, tread firm and ensure that the graft union is above ground. Keep the trunks of wall trees 4 inches away from the walls. Fan trees should be tied temporarily until the soil has settled, bush trees should be staked, putting the stake in the planting hole before the tree. Planting distances are: for fan trees 15 feet apart, and for bush trees 15–20 feet.

Black currants Though most varieties are self-compatible there is greater certainty of good regular yields if more than one variety is grown. Varieties overlap during the flowering season.
Cultivation The modern method of planting black currants is to insert three cuttings 4 inches deep at each planting position and allow them to fruit *in situ*. Plant at 6 × 3 feet intervals. Cuttings 12 inches long, are taken in the autumn from well-ripened shoots of the current season's growth—it is unnecessary to make the cuts directly below the nodes as the cuttings root readily wherever the cuts are made.

Alternatively, plant one to two-year old bushes between October and mid-March, the earlier the better. The soil should be dug deeply prior to planting and have 1 cwt of well-rotted farmyard manure dug in every 10 square yards. Do not allow the fibrous roots to become dry while awaiting planting; heel them in until planting can be carried out. The roots should not have more than 2 inches of soil above them when planted in their permanent positions.

Cuttings rooted *in situ* can be allowed to fruit the first season but transplanted one-year-old bushes should be pruned to help them recover from the transplanting check and induce strong growth, by shortening the shoots to four buds.

Generally, red and white currant bushes are grown with a short leg, 4–5 inches in length, sucker growths being removed; on dry gravel soils, die back may be severe and a multistemmed bush may be more practical. Bushes with a leg are obtained by first removing the buds from the bottom half of each cutting before insertion.

Single or double cordon red or white currants, planted against a wall, give extra-large berries and are easily netted against birds. Plant bushes 5 feet × 5 feet, single cordons 1 foot apart in the row, double cordons, 1½ feet apart in the row; rows 4 feet apart.

Sequence of flowering

Early	Early cont.	Early cont.
Baldwin	brook's Black	Supreme
Blacksmith	Invincible Giant	Wellington XXX
Boskoop Giant	Prolific	Westwick
Cotswold Cross	Laleham Beauty	Choice
Daniel's	Laxton's Giant	Westwick
September	Malvern Cross	Triumph
French Black in-	Mendip Cross	**Late**
cluding Sea-	Raven	Amos Black

Red currants

Early	Late
Earliest of Fourlands	Wilson's Long Bunch
Fay's Prolific	
Laxton's No. 1	
Red Lake	

Varieties normally grown are self-compatible

24

1 A fine crop of Black Currant 'Laxton's Giant'. Though most varieties are self-compatible, better yields are obtained if more than one variety is grown.
2 Gooseberry 'Leveller', an old reliable variety, after picking.

Gooseberries

Early	Early mid cont.	Mid season cont.
Cousen's Seedling	Keepsake	Thatcher
May Duke	Langley Gage	White Lion
Warrington	Whinham's Industry	Whitesmith
Early mid	**Mid season**	**Mid season Late**
Bedford Red	Bedford Yellow	Careless
Crown Bob	Broom Girl	Green Gem
Green Gage	Early Sulphur	
Gunner	Lancashire Lad	**Late**
Ingall's Prolific Red	Leveller	Howard's Lancer (Lancer)
	Speedwell	

Varieties normally grown are self-compatible but there is variation in flowering from district to district

Planting is carried out from November to February on ground previously enriched with farmyard manure. Bushes should be set out 4–6 feet apart each way; single, double and triple cordons at 1 foot, 1½ feet and 2 feet respectively; standards at 4–6 feet apart.

Strawberries Though most popular varieties are self-compatible and can be grown alone, there are two sometimes grown; Oberschlesien and Tardive de Leopold which must be pollinated by varieties flowering at the same time. There is great variation in flowering from one district to another.

Flowering of strawberries

Early	Mid season	Late
Cambridge Favourite	Cambridge Forerunner	Cambridge Rearguard
Cambridge Premier	Cambridge Prizewinner	Merton Princess
Cambridge Profusion	Cambridge Vigour	Sir Joseph Paxton
Cambridge Rival	Early Cambridge	Talisman
Deutsch Evern	Fenland Wonder	
Huxley	Red Gauntlet	
Madam Lefebre	Royal Sovereign	
Perle de Prague		

Planting Strawberries are usually planted in beds, the rows being 2½ to 3 feet apart, the plants 15 to 18 inches apart in the rows, according to the richness of soil. One reason for early soil preparation is that the soil should be firm.

Summer-fruiting strawberries may be planted either in the late summer to early autumn or even in the spring, provided that in the latter instance all blossom is removed the first summer. The earlier plants can go out, the bigger and stronger plants they will make their first year—so, if you can obtain plants so early, plant in July, August, or even September, but October is late.

Strawberry 'Royal Sovereign' comes into fruit fairly early in the season.

The perpetual-fruiting varieties can also be planted in autumn but rooted runners are not available so early. However, as they have time to catch up in spring, October planting is quite satisfactory, provided the soil is properly workable and will break down to a friable tilth. On cold, heavy soils the planting of perpetual strawberries is probably better deferred until spring.

When ordering, for preference stipulate plants which have been rooted in pots. These will be slightly more expensive but they will transplant more readily, with less root damage, and they will have better root development.

Use a trowel for planting and take a hole out for each plant deep enough to accommodate the roots without bending them. Then return a little soil at the centre of the hole to make a mound on which the strawberry plant can 'sit' with its roots spread evenly around it.

The base of the crown should be just at soil level: if it is too high, roots are exposed and dry out, resulting in eventual death of the plant; while if the crown is half buried, it will either produce unwanted weak secondary growths or rot away entirely.

Plant firmly, using the handle of the trowel as a rammer. As you proceed, see that the roots of plants awaiting their turn are not exposed to the wind. Finally, rake the bed smooth and give a good watering to settle the soil.

Raspberries May be planted either in the open or against a fence or wall. In the latter case, the canes can be secured simply by lengths of strong string tied to staples at the ends of the row and at intervals of 18 inches or so. A free-standing row, however, will require substantial posts at each end of the row and these should be put in before planting. Concrete or angle-iron posts make a good permanent job and should be embedded in concrete. Struts should be arranged on the inner sides of the posts to take the strain. Two lengths of gauge 12 or 14 galvanised wire will be required at 2 feet and at 4 feet from the ground (or 5 feet where very vigorous varieties are planted). The canes should be planted 2 feet apart in the row and, if more than one row is wanted, rows should be 6 feet apart.

Raspberries

Early	Late
Lloyd George	Norfolk Giant
Malling Exploit	
Malling Jewel	
Malling Promise	

Popular varieties are self-compatible

Clean fruits Fruit grown to be enjoyed should look good as well as taste good. The appearance and quality of fruit can be marred by certain insect pests and diseases. Steps must be taken to keep these enemies under control and this does not always mean using sprays and dusts.

Insects and fungi are found in some degree on many plants. They become troublesome only when the plants are attacked in sufficient numbers to cause damage. The fact that pests and diseases have alternate wild host plants, makes their control all the more difficult.

When the ground is being prepared for

Raspberry 'Malling Exploit' is a vigorously growing plant and comes into fruit early in the season.

planting, a careful watch should be kept for soil pests such as chafer grubs which eat the roots of young plants. Old tree stumps and similar rubbish can harbour armillaria disease (honey fungus) which can spread in the soil and kill roots. Perennial as well as annual weeds can act as hosts for a number of diseases and certain viruses can be carried in this way and attack the fruit plants. Clean ground before planting is the foundation for future control measures when the plants are growing and cropping. Various soil insecticides and fungicides are available but should be used with care, as they could leave harmful residues in the ground.

Even if the plants put into the ground

are basically healthy, troubles from outside are bound to appear. It is when the plants are growing and making new shoots, leaves, flowers and fruits, that most of the pests and diseases appear. Among insect pests the two biggest culprits are the aphids or greenfly, which in the many forms and colours suck sap from the plants, and the various caterpillars which have a great appetite for any plant material. The various aphids attack the plants constantly through the growing season and their eggs are to be found on some part of a tree or bush during the winter. A few species can remain as adults feeding on leaves the year round. Attacks of this pest can quickly build up and cause serious damage to any part of the plant above ground, such as distorted shoots, leaves and fruits and poor flowers. Fortunately sprays are available to give a quick knockdown of the insects and young nymphs. Some of these, known as sap systemics, are taken into the cell and keep killing the insects over a period of weeks. Warm dry weather suits this pest very well and it requires constant vigilance to spot the beginnings of an attack.

Various species of caterpillar can overwinter often some distance from the fruit plants, and from spring to late autumn keep up attacks on all plants. The winter moth group will attack leaves and shoots in spring and early summer while the tortrix group, which includes the codling moth, concentrates on the maturing fruits.

Attacks of caterpillars should be noted as early as possible. There are a number of very good sprays which will keep their numbers down.

Red spider mite, though not a true insect is a pest which during the summer can cripple trees. The adults suck sap from the leaves which turn bronze and in severe attacks cause russeting of the fruits. Prompt spraying of the plants is important when the first tiny red adults are seen on the undersides of the leaves.

Powdery mildews are the most troublesome diseases of fruit, and in summer cover leaves and shoots with a grey-white felt. These diseases, like so many others are carried over from year to year on the plants and once established are difficult to control. Botrytis, a grey mould on soft fruits, is also a real nuisance, spoiling the fruits just as they are ready to pick. Scab on apples and pears spoils the quality of the fruit when picked and, if severe, causes cankers on the wood.

This is a formidable list, but fortunately there are control materials which if used sensibly and according to directions will counteract most pests and diseases.

Though scientists are investigating newer and better ways of producing clean fruit, there are measures of garden hygiene which can be used, especially during the dormant season. Many pests and diseases overwinter on the trees as eggs, caterpillars or adults. All prunings should be burnt as well as any loose bark which can conceal cocoons of the codling moth. Cankerous wounds should be cleaned and treated with healing paint. Grass or weeds around the base of the plants should be kept down. Greasebands applied to the trunks of the trees in autumn will trap adult moths as they climb the trees to lay their eggs. The collection and destruction of diseased and pest-ridden fruits is necessary at all times. Leaves, on the plants or on the ground, can carry disease over the winter and should be gathered and burnt. Spraying in winter with a tar oil spray can have a good cleaning effect and will also kill a number of pests and diseases directly. To guard against damage from small animals—mice, rats, rabbits or hares—and birds attacking buds, use a repellent spray.

When spraying has to be done, especially in spring or early summer, approach the problem sensibly. A wide range of garden sprays are available. Some will control a few pests or disease only. There are, however, certain combined sprays which, if used according to instructions, deal satisfactorily with a wide range of troubles. Spray thoroughly before a pest or disease really gets a hold on the plant. Most sprays are applied at low concentrations, but more use is being made now of higher concentrations. The latter must be used with care to avoid overspraying and damage. Aerosol sprays are also useful but should not be used closer than 1 foot from the plants being sprayed. High volume spraying is safest under garden conditions.

Wind and frost can spoil the foliage, flowers and fruit. Protection from prevailing winds, especially in exposed areas, must be considered. Good air drainage or covering will reduce losses from frost but the problem of cold winds in summer which can cause russetting of the fruits is not easy to overcome.

Fruit pruning

The purpose of pruning is to encourage cropping in an orderly fashion on fruit plants. Some fruit trees or bushes may require no pruning while others respond to some degree of control.

The branches of most fruit plants can, if they are left unpruned, become so tangled that there is utter chaos. The fruits become small, cropping is irregular and pest and disease control becomes increasingly difficult. Drastic measures will have to be taken to put matters right while yields are lost for some years until order is restored.

Pruning is not a magic art, understood and practised by a few green-fingered experts. The principles are simple and, when considered sensibly, amount very much to commonsense. Pruning is the technique of dealing with the way the branches of a fruit plant can be arranged round the main stem or trunk so that each has a fair share of space.

In an unpruned tree only those shoots on the outside get enough light for the leaves which, with the roots, feed the whole tree. If the leaves are poor in size and colour, the buds and fruits which they feed will also be poor. Extra soil feeding will simply make matters worse.

The solution is at least some pruning to let in light. Many gardeners get the impression that pruning is essential for good fruiting. This is not so. The less a tree or plant is cut about, the more fruitful it will be. To some extent nature itself may take a hand as winds and storms may remove a number of branches. However, this unselected removal of shoots may not be completely beneficial, particularly since the main branches may be broken at the crotch where they meet the main stem. Sometimes, too, a temporary attack by a pest or disease reduces growth, but this also may be of uncertain value. Pruning is man's way of improving on nature to get earlier and more regular yields.

All fruit plants are perennial and if kept healthy will crop for many years. Even strawberries will grow and crop longer than their normal garden span of 3–4 years. Soft fruits will come into good cropping a year or two after planting but tree fruits take longer. By using dwarfing rootstocks this interval can be shortened,

Pruning varies according to the plant. Remove the two-year old wood after Black currants have fruited.

Dead, broken or crossing branches are taken from a Plum tree in summer, to admit more light and air.

while vigorous rootstocks delay cropping though yields per tree are greater. Some tree fruits, e.g. sweet cherries may not give worthwhile crops until ten years after planting.

In the garden, fruit plants are valuable assets and we should look after them to avoid disappointment and even despair. If the simple elements of pruning are understood and applied the results are worthwhile.

One of the biggest snags in growing fruit is that the bushes are often planted too close together and suffer from competition. Drastic pruning would in many instances be wrong. Complete removal of some of the plants, and the containment by pruning of those that remain, would be the best proposition. Again, choice of rootstock can play an important part. Pruning aims to use the characteristics of the varieties and the rootstock, together with soil management, to produce a fruiting plant with adequately spaced branches and shoots, to achieve a sensible balance between growth and cropping and to remove old and sometimes diseased shoots and replace them with new growth.

While the basic principles of pruning are the same for all fruits, their interpretation and application may vary, depending on a number of factors. The effects of soil and situation on the plants must be taken into account and in one garden or orchard there are differences between varieties of one kind of fruit as well as between each kind. We do not prune a black currant bush as we would a sweet cherry or a bush apple as we would a cordon. Each type and variety needs a slightly different approach and

1

2

3

5

4

1 Pears are pruned in July or August to encourage the formation of fruit buds for the following spring.
2 The side growths are shortened to about five leaves from the base.
3 Old Black currant bushes can be treated drastically and cut right back.
4 The regrowth is quite thick.
5 The weaker and overcrowded shoots are removed by hand to reduce the number.

---

possibly even opposite treatment to achieve good results.

To understand what happens when a fruit plant is pruned, it is worth understanding a little about how it grows.

Plants are made up of a collection of cells. Some of these cells do special things. The tough outer skin or bark is for protection. Underneath are the bast cells to transfer food to all parts, the active living or cambium cells, and the wood cells to transport water, and the inner scaffolding cells for support. All these work together and are interconnected so that the plants develop properly.

Raw food materials including water are taken up from the soil by the roots and root hairs into the branches where the leaves, with the help of light and air, transform them into sugar, starches, proteins and oils needed by the plant for sturdy growth. This emphasises the importance of good leaves and, within reason, the more there are the better for fruiting.

In many gardens and orchards one of the first acts of pruning may be to let in light and air by removing some unwanted branches e.g. those that are dead or badly diseased, crossing the centre of the tree, or even too near the ground. This action may seem to be obvious and if not overdone in one season can work wonders.

The majority of the best fruits are to be found on the younger branches, with most of the smaller and low quality fruits on older wood. This younger wood is generally to be found towards the outside of the plant and will have larger and better green leaves, which will feed the fruit buds. These in turn give better flowers and more certain crops or larger fruits. On older branches the leaves tend to be small and of poorer colour, also fewer in number. Thus the renewal or replacement of old or ageing branches tend to keep up the production of high-quality fruit.

When considering the pruning of any fruit tree the following points are worth noting:
(a) Cut out dead or diseased wood, also broken and overcrowding branches.
(b) Encourage a moderate amount of young growth and stimulate this in stunted and backward plants.
(c) Where the number of fruit buds is excessive reduce them.

Pruning of apples Most apple trees are purchased when they are 1–4 years old. Trees older than this will need special care to help them over the shock of transplanting. A good nurseryman ensures that the trees he sends out have healthy strong shoots, properly spaced for the type of tree which is to be grown —bush, cordon, pyramid or any other shape.

The gardener who wishes to train his own trees will plant maidens. These are one-year-old trees with a single stem, possibly with a few sideshoots, called feathers. This is the cheapest way of buying a tree. There is no reason why the first pruning should not be done in the winter of planting and this is a time to decide what type of tree should be grown. A selection can be made from the following.

A standard tree is one with a 6 foot long stem. These are not suitable for gardens as they make large trees, which are

1 Pruning tools: 1, **Saw,** 2, **Parrot-nosed Saw,** 3, **Budding Knife,** 4, **Pruning Knife,** 5, 6 and 7, **types of Secateur.**
2 A maiden Apple tree, staked to prevent rocking in the wind.

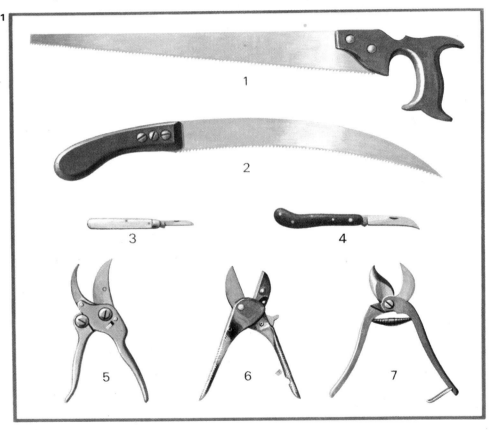

1

2

3

4

5

6

7

32

difficult to manage. They can, however, make pleasant shade trees. The early treatment of the standard tree consists in pruning the maiden after planting, removing half to one third of its length to encourage a further upright shoot to form a main stem at 6 feet.

The tree should, at one year after planting, be tall enough to prune this main stem so that the lowest branch is at the right height from ground level.

Pruning thereafter may consist simply of the removal of overcrowding branches with the occasional pruning of the ends of the leading shoots to help to form new growth.

Spurs, which are shoots with a number of fruit buds, can be reduced in size, since too many fruit buds can be as embarrassing as too few. In spite of very light pruning some varieties on vigorous rootstocks may take 10–12 years before giving a decent crop. Suitable rootstocks for standard trees are M.XVI and M.XXV.

The half-standard tree has a main stem of 4½–5 feet. It is more manageable than a standard tree in the early years, but varieties on a vigorous stock still make big heads with delayed cropping. Half standard trees on medium vigorous stocks e.g. M.II or MM.111 could be very useful in gardens where other plants are grown underneath and not too big a tree is useful. Pruning is similar to that for a standard tree. The maiden can be pruned at 5–5½ feet from ground level in the year of planting and the shoots which grow the following summer form the basis of the branch system. Most varieties will grow and crop happily with the minimum of pruning even on medium

2

vigorous rootstocks which usually encourage earlier cropping — 6–8 years from planting.

Large bush trees growing about 15–18 feet high, are popular in large gardens. The main stem is 2½–3 feet long. The lowest branches make cropping underneath difficult except for grass. Varieties growing on medium vigorous rootstocks

M.II, M.VII, M.IV, MM.104, MM.106 and MM.101 do very well. The trees can be managed fairly easily from ground level. Pruning starts with the maiden which is pruned at a point 3–3½ feet from ground level. As a result of this pruning a number of shoots, possibly three to five, will grow from the buds below the pruning cut in the following summer. The shoot from the topmost bud (the leader) should be fairly upright, while the remainder become less upright the lower down the stem they are.

If a feathered maiden is planted (and these may be a little dearer than a plain maiden), many of the shoots that will form from the first branches are already there.

Pruning of the main stem in this instance is simply to add a few more shoots as spares and possibly to balance the tree, so that there is even distribution of branches. It is possible at this stage to distribute the main branches over 2–3 feet of stem above the lowest branch by continuing to prune the central lead for two years after planting.

This will form a delayed open centre tree which is less subject to loss of main branches than the open centre tree where all branches come off at one level. During this period the side branches (laterals) may receive some treatment. If growth is vigorous it would be wise not to prune those that are well positioned round the main stem. If there are too many, and five to seven should be ample, cut out the remainder close to the main stem. The unpruned shoots will make further extension growth and possibly, depending on variety and continued vigour, a number of useful sideshoots.

These unpruned shoots should flower and fruit well three to five years after planting and, other factors being favourable, the tree should be cropping fully four to five years later. This is termed the regulated system of pruning and can be applied to many varieties.

Where the amount of new extension growth falls below 12–15 inches, pruning and possibly soil feeding will be needed to encourage growth. On any branch or tree which is not making the necessary amount of growth, prune the leaders, removing a half to one third of their length. The same treatment is advised for varieties which tend to form fruit buds on the ends of the young shoots (tip bearers). There will come a time, even with the regulated tree, when one or two branches may have to be cut out and some provision can be made to renew older branches, possibly from nearer the middle of the tree.

Another system is to provide for the replacement of older branches by building up a system of renewal shoots, which can take over cropping when needed. In this way there can always be a supply of young growth in the tree for maximum quality cropping.

Over a period of twenty years much of the tree may have been renewed two to three times. A renewal branch should be carefully selected from shoots growing directly from an existing branch, and should be some five to six years younger than the branch it will replace. There will be occasions when it is necessary to replace an oldish branch by a renewal shoot from a neighbouring branch.

A notable characteristic of unpruned or lightly pruned apple trees is that the branches tend to grow outwards instead of upwards. Where the trees are pruned hard the branches tend to be very upright and difficult to control.

This is important, since near-horizontal branches are more fruitful than upright growing shoots. The weight of crop and leaves will also bring branches down and it is not unusual to find branches of trees weighted or tied down.

Within the tree itself, any unwanted branches or shoots are best cut out completely. Strong growths, known as water shoots, appearing mainly on the crotch area, should be taken out at any

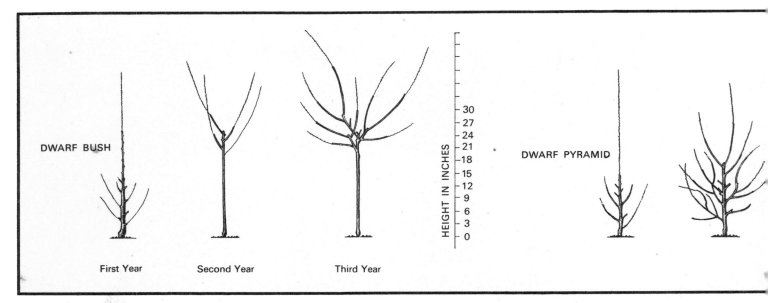

DWARF BUSH

First Year   Second Year   Third Year

HEIGHT IN INCHES

30
27
24
21
18
15
12
9
6
3
0

DWARF PYRAMID

time of the year. Similarly, branches that are growing too upright can be cut down to lower and more horizontal branches. If too many young shoots form on fruiting branches a number, e.g. one third, can be removed completely, a further third left full length, and the remainder shortened to 6–9 inches. These last will help to form spurs with fruit buds or a further supply of new shoots. While these proportions will vary from tree to tree the method is a means of keeping up a succession of young fruiting wood. The formation of fruit buds on spurs—natural from existing fruit buds or artificial by pruning—can account for 70% of the fruiting area on an apple tree. Good quality varieties which spur naturally have an advantage over those which need encouragement by pruning. This quality of free spurring can, if carried too far, as in a neglected tree, bring trouble—not enough new growth, too many small fruits.

Unless a large bush tree has been sadly neglected or is suffering from lack of feeding it should manage very well with a moderate amount of winter pruning. If for some reason too much growth is being made, summer pruning in July or tying down of upright branches should help.

Dwarfing bushes are very popular in the garden. Varieties grafted or budded on semi-dwarfing rootstocks need not exceed 7 feet in height. A number of varieties on these stocks can be even smaller. At their heights the trees are easy to manage and can be planted fairly close together. Suitable rootstocks are dwarfing M.IX and M.IXA, semi-dwarfing M.26.

One feature of rootstock influence on such bushes is the encouragement to produce early fruit bud formation. Pruning is not necessary to bring this about. It often happens that because there are too many fruit buds, hard pruning is necessary to keep the plants growing and a number of the buds may have to be taken off. Unless this is done, too many fruits are formed.

The maiden tree is pruned at 2–2½ feet

Patterns of pruning to build a dwarf bush tree, dwarf pyramid and cordon, from a one-year old tree, or maiden.

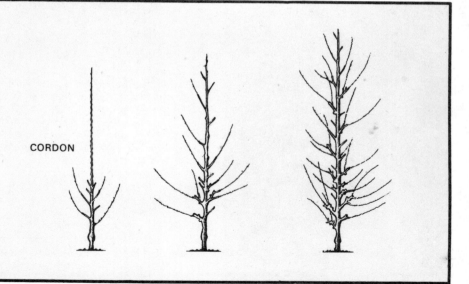

CORDON

from ground level after planting. The three to five branches which grow during the following summer are pruned again in the following winter removing about one half to one third of the length, depending on vigour, but in such a way that there is an even spread of vigour and branches round each plant. At this stage there are probably enough branches to see the tree through its whole life. In the following years more and more fruit buds and spurs appear and good cropping takes place 4–5 years after planting. Not many surplus shoots will appear on the branches and those can be shortened to 2–3 buds from the branches.

When cropping really starts some fruit bud reduction can be made. It is worth noting that each fruit bud can produce 4–5 fruitlets and gross over-crowding can result. This happens especially with free spurring varieties. It is a simple matter to remove surplus buds in winter by hand. With finger and thumb pinch out the upper leaf of some buds and push others out completely.

Allow 4–6 inches between fruit buds or spurs. If there are a number of fruit buds together or on spurs leave one untouched, pinch out two and rub out the remainder. Pinching will remove the flower but still allow leaves to form and probably one or two young shoots. Leaf numbers and quality are important if good sized fruits are to form on the buds that remain untouched. The proportion should be about one. fruit to thirty

A clean cut cannot be achieved unless the branch is cut from underneath. A tear admits fungus diseases.

leaves.

It will be necessary during the cropping life of these small bushes to prune the ends of the leaders to encourage a little new extension growth each year. If new growth is less than 6 inches, cut half the length of the shoot. Tip-bearing varieties e.g. 'Worcester Pearmain' and free budding varieties e.g. 'Lane's Prince Albert' will need pruning, in the one instance to form a yearly supply of new shoots and to avoid bare stems, and in the other to reduce the number of buds and encourage some growth. These treatments may seem drastic but it is known that only about 5% of all the flowers on a tree need be pollinated to set a full crop.

When the spurs become rather large they can be reduced in size to a few buds only or if there is overcrowding a few can be removed completely.

Pyramid shaped trees are also small bushes on dwarfing or semi-dwarfing stocks. They are very useful in small gardens as they can be kept compact. The maiden tree is pruned to within 18 inches from ground level after planting.

In the following winter each new leader is pruned to 10 inches, depending on vigour, above the cut made in the previous winter.

The direction of the top bud at each cut should be varied so that an upright main stem is made. When this reaches about 7 feet high—and this may take many years, if ever—the top can be removed in mid summer to restrict new growth.

While the main stem is growing, side-shoots have grown round it. Space these branches about 6–8 inches apart round the stem and cut out the remainder.

Those left should not, if possible, overlap each other. They are encouraged to form a few more branches by pruning, removing a third to one half of the length in the first winter after planting. Any branch which is rather upright should be tied to a near horizontal position. This should have the effect of restricting growth and encouraging fruit buds to form. Pruning of shoots (laterals) in the following years should be as light as possible, the aim being to restrict the spread of branches to about 18–24 inches from the main stem. If too much extension growth is made, carry out summer pruning of offending shoots in June or July, when they are about 6–9 inches long—simply pinch out the end of each shoot. Again, if there are too many branch laterals in any year these should also be rubbed out in summer, allowing 9–12 inches between those that remain. With little or no winter pruning for growth and summer pruning to restrict growth, fruit buds and spurs should form freely on most varieties. It will be necessary to remove a number of these in a similar fashion as for bush trees to avoid over-cropping and crowding of branches.

The pillar shape of small tree is in some respects similar to the pyramid. The central stem is formed in the same way and the height restricted to 6½–7 feet. The main difference is in the treatment of the side branches, none of which last more than three seasons. The pruning of

1 Saw branches off close to the main stem.
2 Paint wounds with Arbrex or lead paint.
3 The cordon system provides an intensive, yet decorative way of growing fruit.

these is based on the way the fruit buds usually form. A young shoot grows one summer and forms pointed wood or growth buds. The second summer the shoots form plump fruit buds, which in the following, or third, summer flower and bear fruits. If the shoot is not pruned, some buds will form in the first summer to flower and fruit the next year. If a shoot is not pruned during this three-year period it should carry most of its best fruits in the third summer. The system works as follows: all the three to four sideshoots formed round the main stem when the maiden is pruned 18 inches from ground level after planting are allowed to grow unpruned for three years. These shoots bear fruits in the third summer, and in the winter following are cut back to about 1 inch from the main stem. On this stump there are a number of dormant wood buds which in the following summer grow to form new shoots. The number arising from each stump should be restricted to two and the remainder rubbed out in summer.

The two shoots left in are allowed to grow for three seasons and then pruned back to 1 inch as before. This sequence of pruning is carried out farther up the tree as new branches develop, until all the branches are being replaced on a three year basis, resulting in young wood and good crops. As the trees are planted close in the rows, it pays to prune each fruit bud bearing shoot in the second winter at the last fruit bud. This reduces overcrowding, thus letting light and air into the young shoots. It may even be necessary to cut out completely any surplus two-year shoots. In time the 1 inch stumps to which the fruit branches are cut back, become rather large and are cut back after 3–4 years to 1 inch from the main stem to form a fresh supply of new shoots.

Pillar trees in full growth and cropping may look rather untidy but they crop well. Use a dwarfing or semi-dwarfing rootstock to help control the vigorous growth resulting from rather hard pruning.

The spindle bush is another type of tree with a central leader and controlled to about 7 feet in height. The main stem is formed in the same way as for pyramid and pillar.

The side branches are left unpruned. To encourage early cropping, these shoots are looped round and tied to the main stem or even suitable neighbouring branches. These branches can be left unpruned for 3–4 years and be replaced completely, as in the pillar tree, or reduced in length to be replaced by young shoots over a period of two years. The basis of this tree form is the continuing replacement of wood which has cropped well for at least one year—but possibly three—by younger potential wood and the bending of these shoots from the first year to bear early heavy crops. The loops should not be too tight and the trees may have to be reviewed each year. It is an untidy but profitable tree shape. Dwarfing and semi-dwarfing rootstocks are used.

Cordon forms of tree have been tried very successfully for many years and each takes up very little space. They can be grown against a wall or wire framework in the open. Using this method a fair number of varieties can be grown in a small area and the trees are easily managed. Single cordons, consisting of one main stem are the most common form. The cordons can either be upright or at an angle, when they are known as oblique cordons. The latter is preferred.

The maiden is planted against its support at an angle of 45°. Pruning of the leading shoot may or may not be necessary and depends on variety, rootstock and soil.

With a semi-vigorous rootstock on good soil the main stem will grow happily without pruning and form enough sideshoots. With a dwarfing or semi-dwarfing root-stock, even on a good soil, very light leader pruning is advised to encourage new extension growth and enough sideshoots. At the most, cut off the top 3 inches of the leader, or none at all if growth is good. In the course of a few years the main stem will reach the top of the support, some 6½–7 feet. At this stage it can be cut away from the support and lowered to 30° so that further extension growth is possible. During this time sideshoots have grown and their growth should be controlled quite strictly, as each cordon is only 2–3 feet from its neighbour. It is possible to contain the growth by summer pruning in June or July, when the shoots are pencil thickness, and about 12 inches long. On plants growing in the open these shoots, about twelve for each year of growth are distributed round the stem. With trees trained against a wall, shoots growing towards the wall are removed. Each shoot left on the tree is summer pruned to 6 inches. A number of buds below the cut should form fruit buds, but some will grow in late summer; this is known as secondary growth. In

A triple cordon Apple grown against a wall to utilise a small space.

the following winter the spurs so made can be shortened to three or four fruit buds from the base, or left alone if space allows. At the same time any other shoots can be left full length or cut back if more than 12 inches long.

Each year during the life of the tree this system of summer and winter pruning is used. If natural or artificial spurs become too big they can be reduced in size and number of fruit buds to avoid overcropping and shading of younger buds. Two good fruit buds to each spur will give ample flowers.

A modification of the cordon is to encourage young shoots, not spurs, to develop, and to loop these to encourage fruit buds to form, and when these are cropped to replace them with a fresh set. *The espalier shape* of tree is one with a central stem 6½–7 feet high and with a number of equally spread branches coming away from it in pairs. The maiden tree is pruned to within 18 inches of ground level after planting. The following year a pair of opposite branches is selected and tied horizontally.

The upright leader is pruned again at 18 inches and a further pair of side branches selected the following winter, approximately 15 inches above the first pair and in the same plane. In the following two winters the treatment is repeated so that there are four pairs of horizontal branches five years after planting. The leader on the main stem is suppressed in the sixth summer by summer pruning. During this shaping period the older side branches have been

39

growing horizontally.

Leader growth will be moderate only and leader pruning not necessary unless extension and lateral growth is backward.

Fruit bud formation should take place easily and the general scheme of pruning on each side branch will follow the same pattern as for cordons. Spur pruning and removal of surplus fruit buds will be routine.

In a modification of this shape, the

The arcure system of training apple trees is a series of arches. One strong shoot is left to develop at the apex of each arch, to form the arch above. The new growth is arched over in July, when any necessary pruning is done.

centre leader is stopped at 15 inches from ground level and the branches trained in an upright position to form 'U' and double 'U' espaliers. This type of tree shape is very compact and fruitful. Semi-dwarfing or semi-vigorous rootstocks should be used.

The palmette tree shape is a modified espalier. The basis of this system is still a central leader trained against a support. From this main stem there are numbers of branches in the same plane. These branches, which need not be in pairs, are spaced about 12 inches apart and looped on to the supports. Any of the branches can be replaced partly or wholly and retrained on to the supports. In this way a succession of young fruiting wood is maintained in the tree.

Crop yields can be very good from this system. Use semi-dwarfing or semi-vigorous rootstocks.

Arcure is a system in which the tree is trained on a trellis in a succession of arcs. The maiden tree is bent over and one strong shoot from it is allowed to grow from the centre of the arc and is in turn bent over in the opposite direction. The process is repeated each year until the top of the support is reached and further upward growth is suppressed by summer pruning. As the branches age they can be replaced or retained and a system of spurs developed and treated as any other spurs.

Choose dwarfing or semi-dwarfing rootstocks.

Pruning of pears Pears are pruned in very much the same fashion as apples but most varieties grow rather vigorously as young plants. Quince A or B rootstocks,

on which most trees are grafted, have only limited control over growth. It is usually difficult to control the strong upright growth of the trees and weighting or tying is used to bring the branches down to a horizontal position. When cropping does begin, however, growth slows down and fruit buds and spurs appear in abundance. At this stage the problem is often to encourage young growth in the tree.

During the first two winters after

A newly planted fan-trained plum. The branches will be tied to canes which are fixed to the horizontal wires.

planting a maiden tree, the leaders, the main extension shoots, are pruned, removing a half to two thirds of their length each winter. This will encourage sideshoots to develop as well as form the main branches. After the second winter enough branches should have formed and these should be weighted or tied towards the horizontal. With certain trained types of shapes—cordons, espaliers and palmettes this is straightforward.

As pear varieties tend to develop buds which either remain small, dormant or undeveloped blind buds, some pruning of laterals should be carried out. It may be sufficient to remove only the end third of a lateral growth. Unpruned shoots in a tree seldom remain productive for long.

The great majority of pear varieties respond to spur pruning as for apples. Sideshoots are cut back to three to four buds. Two varieties 'Jargonelle' and 'Joséphine de Malines' are tip bearers, with the fruit buds forming on the ends of shoots, and pruning is needed to keep up a supply.

As the trees grow and fill the space given to them there can be a gradual replacing of old branches with younger ones. Very upright branches can be cut back to lower and more horizontal branches. Spur size numbers on a branch can be reduced to let in light, otherwise blind buds occur.

Most of the popular varieties of pears can be grown in the same tree shapes as apples but standards or half-standards are not recommended.

Plums, gages and damsons In many gardens these are planted as maidens and grown as half-standard trees with 4–5 foot stems. Growth is rapid in the first few years. Nurserymen can supply trees already pruned with 3–5 branches. March is the best time to prune these fruits, when growth is beginning.

During the succeeding years the trees should grow quite happily with the minimum of pruning, apart from cutting out—again in spring or after fruit picking—broken, dead or diseased branches and any that have over-reached themselves.

With drooping varieties e.g. 'Early Laxton' or 'Victoria', prune to upward growing buds or shoots. Upright varieties should be pruned to outward pointing buds or shoots.

Fan-trained trees are popular but their formation is a skilled job. Many gardeners prefer to plant trees already shaped. The maiden tree is pruned to 18–24 inches from ground level in the winter of planting. Two or more shoots grow the following summer. Select two growths opposite each other and about 12–15 inches from ground level. These are trained outwards at an angle of 45°.

In the following March each of the shoots is pruned to 15–18 inches from the main stem. In the summer there is a further supply of shoots and three or four are chosen to train outwards and upwards to make a fan. In the third spring after planting, each selected shoot is pruned to about 2 feet from its point of growth. The amount of growth made the following summer should suffice to cover a reasonable framework.

Fruit production on the older part of the fan has been started on one-year-old unpruned shoots distributed about 6 inches apart in the line of the branches.

Any surplus is cut out completely. Only if the selected shoots exceed 18 inches in length are they pruned, to avoid excessive shading. This is done in summer when disbudding, pinching and tying are the principal tasks.

As growth begins in early summer, select the best place near the base of an existing shoot and which it will replace. Remove any other near by when quite small. A space of 6 inches between each fruiting shoot may seem a lot in winter but in summer it looks very close. After fruit picking remove the fruited shoot and tie in the new one.

Peaches, nectarines and apricots These stone fruits can be grown as large bushes or as trained trees in the open. However they are grown, pruning is done either in spring or late summer. The pruning of bush trees is very similar to that given to plums.

Maidens are pruned at 2 feet from soil level and 3–5 branches are selected to form the basic shape of the bush and the surplus removed completely. Any further pruning need consist only of removing dead tips and dead and overcrowding branches. This pruning can be done in August or September. Half-standard trees on 3½–4 foot stems are pruned in a similar fashion. If too much summer growth is made, cut out surplus shoots leaving the remainder 6 inches apart. These fruits are also commonly fan-trained (see Plums above).

Sweet cherries These are grown as standards or half-standards and grafted or budded on to a vigorous rootstock. Standards have a 5–6 foot stem and half-standards 3½–4 foot. The maiden is pruned at the selected height in the spring after planting.

The result will be 3–4 strong branches and unless growth is hampered by other factors, this should suffice for some years. If crossing, overhanging or dead branches appear these should be cut out in spring or late summer.

Duke cherries are less vigorous than sweet varieties and with similar pruning are more useful in gardens.

Acid (sour) cherries make useful standards. Pruning after the early maiden treatment consists of keeping a supply of one-year shoots on which fruiting takes place the following year. Prune to replace about one-third of the growth in the tree each August after picking as well as dead, diseased and overcrowding shoots.

Figs After planting, fig trees should grow away very happily and often become very untidy. Since full sunlight is essential if the fruits are to mature, drastic removal of unwanted growths is done in the period June to August. The plants will stand up to this hard pruning, provided a number of fruiting spurs are left in. Long sappy growths are cut back hard each autumn.

Hazelnuts and filberts (cobs) Young, 2–3 year old plants are pruned after planting. Each of the leaders is pruned by half for a year or two to form a branch system. After this the laterals are pruned in early winter to form spurs, about 12 inches from the main stem. As the spurs become too large they can be reduced in size. They are grown as dwarf

Rasperries in late March, tied in to supporting wires.

bushes with about 10–12 main branches and about 5 feet high.

Raspberries Fruit is formed on canes which grew the year before. During the summer the canes make branchlets on which flowers and fruits form. After picking, the canes and leaves turn brown. These canes are cut close to ground level and burnt. Young canes from the ground will take over next season. Young plants are cut to 3–4 buds from ground level after planting. In the following summer a few fruiting laterals will grow from these buds but new canes will grow from the ground to start cropping the year after.

A healthy established plant will produce up to twelve new canes each

year. If all are kept in there would be overcrowding, so only the best 4–6 are kept and the rest cut to ground level with the old canes. The new canes are tied to a support and any that are too long, bent over and if necessary pruned to the height of the support the following spring. At this time also any tips which have been killed by frost are cut to a healthy bud. Though most varieties fruit in June and July, autumn fruiting can be encouraged by pruning all shoots to ground level in February.

Gooseberries Most gooseberry bushes are already 2–3 years old from cuttings when planted and have already formed branches spaced round the short main stem, known as the leg. Shoots not needed for extension are pruned in February to 1 inch to make spurs.

Future pruning aims to keep the bushes reasonably open and replacing old branches with new. Leading or replacement shoots are pruned by half each year to keep up a supply of side-shoots which are cut to 1 inch. If the plants are really growing well, even leader pruning can be dispensed with, but weak-growing plants may need more drastic treatment and feeding.

Cut out old, weak or dead shoots and with drooping varieties prune to upward pointing shoots or buds. Bushes growing in exposed areas should have more shoots left in them than those growing in shelter.

Gooseberries can be grown as cordons, restricting the number of main growths to one, two or three. The selected leading shoots are pruned hard each winter until they reach the top of the support. Sideshoots are pruned to 1 inch to form spurs. Pruning of plants grown as stools without a leg simply consists in cutting out surplus shoots from all types to keep the plants open. As birds can damage buds, a repellent spray should be used as a precaution from mid January onwards.

Blackberries and loganberries Fruiting takes place mainly on young shoots which grew in the previous year. A few varieties, e.g. 'John Innes Berry' form fruits on two-year-old shoots.

Young plants are pruned to 3–4 buds after planting, and the strong shoots which grow are tied to suitable supports to fruit the year after. In the following years new shoots will grow on old wood and also come from ground level. After

Red currant 'Laxton's No. 1' is an early fruiting variety, which bears a good crop of berries.

fruiting, cut out as much of the old wood as possible and train in the new shoots. If there are too many, remove the surplus completely. With the weaker growing loganberries, 6–8 new canes each year should cover the framework. Shoots growing above the framework can be arched over and if need be, pruned in spring.

These fruits can be trained as fans, spread over the framework. New canes are looped along the lowest wire as they grow and then in autumn take the place of the old.

Black currants These are grown as stools after planting. Young plants raised from cuttings are cut to 2–3 buds from ground level after planting. The shoots which grow in the first summer will fruit the year after. In succeeding years pruning, which can be hard or light depending on growth, aims to keep up a supply of new shoots. This will mean the cutting out of a proportion of old, unfruitful wood (and some young shoots). Prune the older shoots as close to ground level as possible. It is possible to grow plants against a framework and the techniques are the same as for bushes but the branches are tied to suitable supports. Pruning should be done as soon as the fruit is picked or in winter.

Red and white currants Young plants from the nursery are usually 2–3 years old and the main branches are already formed on a short leg. After planting the leading shoots are pruned by half to two-thirds depending on vigour. The laterals, or side branches, are pruned in winter to 1 inch from the main stem.

From time to time old branches can be replaced by new growth lower down. Resist the temptation to keep too many shoots in the mature plants, 8–12 should be ample.

These currants can also be trained as cordons with one, two or three branches. The shoots from the young plants are trained to a suitable framework. The leader is pruned hard, removing half to two-thirds of the length until the required height is reached. Laterals in the meantime are pruned to 1 inch from the main stem to form spurs which are thinned out from time to time.

Fan-shaped bushes are also useful. The five or six branches from young shoots are spread on a suitable support and trained as cordons.

Standard red currants and gooseberries One-year-old plants from the cutting rows can be trained to make standard bushes with a main stem of 2½–3 feet. One shoot, usually the topmost, is retained and encouraged to grow upright to form the main stem. At the desired height it is pruned above a good bud to begin the branch system the following year. It may take three to four years before a main stem framework branches are made, especially with weak varieties. The pruning of the head of the standard thereafter follows the same lines as a bush. Greater care should be taken to avoid overcrowding of branches especially with vigorous varieties. Staking should be done early, as the plants may in time become top-heavy. It may be possible to purchase standards grafted on the sturdier *Ribes aureum* as the rootstock.

Fruit picking and storing

Berried fruits are picked when fully ripe for dessert use, or slightly under-ripe for culinary purposes. Early thinnings of gooseberries can be cooked, leaving the remainder to enlarge to dessert size. Soft fruits cannot be stored; freezing or cooking is necessary.

Raspberries are picked to leave the fruit plug on the plant. Strawberries are plugged after picking. Black and red currants are harvested as whole trusses. Mulberries may be allowed to fall from the tree when ripe on to a polythene sheet laid on the ground. Sweet cherries are picked by the cluster; Morello cherries should be cut off with scissors to avoid brown rot infection of the spurs.

Peaches must be palmed off—without using finger-tip pressures. Test each fruit on the tree for ripeness by holding it in the palm of the hand and giving a slight tug. Place ripe peaches on a bed of wadding.

Apples and pears must be handled carefully if bruising is to be avoided. Pick apples when the fruit parts readily from the spur when raised to a horizontal position and twisted slightly. An increasing amount of windfalls is a reminder that the crop is due for picking.

Cooking apples can be picked over when large enough to handle, leaving the remaining fruits to grow on.

Most pears should be gathered in a semi-ripe condition. Pears allowed to ripen on the tree go 'sleepy' in store; pears picked too early shrivel. Pick early and mid-season pears when the green colour is just changing to yellow. Use the lifting test for late pears. All fruits should be dry at picking time.

Special canvas picking buckets fitted with shoulder straps and having a quick release base are useful where a large quantity of fruit is to be picked. On a domestic scale, polythene buckets are preferable to galvanised pails. Never use wicker baskets as these are liable to scar the fruit.

The question of fruit storage is important and often deserves more attention than it receives from amateur gardeners. It is necessary to prepare a proper place with suitable conditions in which to store fruit at harvest time. There is

Picking good clean strawberries from plants mulched with straw. Harvesting fruit should always be done during dry weather, if possible.

no point in growing good fruit if it is allowed to rot away before being eaten. In this country of course we are mainly concerned with apples and pears because we have little else which will keep for long which is grown in great quantity.

Allow harvested apples to sweat for a couple of days before putting them on the storage racks.

Wrapping apples in oiled paper prolongs their storage life, maintains quality and prevents rotting fruit infecting adjacent apples. Newspaper wraps are better than nothing.

Storing apples in polythene sleeves, with a rubber band between each fruit, is a simple method of gas storage—exhaled carbon dioxide retards the ripening process.

White-wood Dutch fruit trays, having short corner posts for easy stacking, are ideal for home storage of fruit. Each holds about 28 lb. Bulk supplies of cooking apples can be stored in clamps with straw bales as walls. Pears should be stored in a single layer for easy examination for condition and ripeness. Store quinces separately from other fruits to avoid the pungent quince aroma being absorbed.

Try to maintain the fruit store at about 37–40°F (3–4°C). Apples need a moist temperature, pears a dry one. An all-purpose fruit store should preferably have an earthen floor to provide even humidity. Straw bales round the walls will insulate the store from frost. Insecticides should be used to keep down

Slatted fruit storage trays allow air to circulate around the fruit. Ideally each fruit should not touch the next.

Apples when to pick and when to eat

Variety	When to pick	Season
Allington Pippin	Late Oct	Oct-Jan
Annie Elizabeth	Mid-Oct	Nov-April
Arthur Turner	End July-Mid Sept	Aug-Nov
Barnack Beauty	Mid Oct	Dec-April
Beauty of Bath	End July onwards	Aug
Belle de Boskoop	Mid Oct	Dec-April
Blenheim Orange	Mid Oct	Nov-Jan
Bramley's Seedling	Late Sept-Mid Oct	Oct-April
Brownlee's Russet	Mid Oct	Jan-April
Charles Ross	Sept	Oct-Nov
Claygate Pearmain	Mid Oct	Dec-Feb
Court Pendu Plat	Early Nov	Nov-May
Cox's Orange Pippin	Late Sept-Early Oct	Oct-Feb
Crawley Beauty	Mid Oct	Dec-April
Crimson Cox	Early Oct	Oct-Feb
Devonshire Quarrenden	Late July onwards	Aug-Sept
Duke of Devonshire	Oct	Feb-March
Early Victoria	When of culinary size	July-Aug
Edward VII	Mid Oct	Dec-April
Egremont Russet	Early Oct	Nov-Dec
Ellison's Orange	Late Sept	Oct-Nov
Emperor Alexander	Mid Sept	Sept-Nov
Epicure	Aug	Sept
Exquisite	Late Aug	Sept-Oct
Fortune	Early Sept	Sept-Nov
Gascoyne's Scarlet	Early Oct	Oct-Jan
Golden Noble	End Sept	Sept-Jan
Golden Spire	End Sept	Sept-Oct
Gravenstein	Late Sept	Oct-Dec
Granny Smith	Leave until frosts	Dec-May
Grenadier	Mid Aug	Aug-Sept
Herring's Pippin	Early Oct	Oct-Nov
Irish Peach	Early Aug	Aug
James Grieve	Early Sept·	Sept-Oct

Variety	When to pick	Season
King of the Pippins	Early Oct	Oct-Nov
Lady Sudeley	Early Aug	Aug-Oct
Lane's Prince Albert	Sept	Nov-March
Laxton's Superb	Mid Oct	Oct-March
Lord Derby	Late Sept	Oct-Dec-Jan
Lord Lambourne	Late Sept	Oct-Nov
May Queen	Oct	Jan-May
Merton Beauty	Early Sept	Sept-Oct
Merton Charm	Early Sept	Sept-Nov
Merton Prolific	Mid Oct	Nov-Feb
Merton Russet	Oct	Jan-March
Merton Worcester	Mid Sept	Sept-Oct
Monarch	Sept-early Oct	Oct-Feb
Mother	Late Sept	Oct-Nov
Newton Wonder	Mid Oct	Dec-March
Orleans Reinette	Mid Oct	Jan-Feb
Peasgood's Nonsuch	Mid Sept	Sept-Nov
Red Ellison	Mid Sept	Oct-Jan
Rev. W. Wilks	Mid Oct	Oct-Nov
Ribston Pippin	Late Sept	Nov-Jan
Rival	Mid Oct	Oct-Dec
St Cecilia	Early Oct	Dec-March
St Edmund's Russet	Early Sept	Sept-Oct
Scarlet Pimpernel	End July	Aug-Sept
Spartan	Mid Oct	Nov-March
Sturmer Pippin	Leave until frosts	Jan-May
Sunset	Mid Oct	Nov-Feb
Tydeman's Early Worcester	Aug	Aug-Sept
Tydeman's Late Orange	Late Oct	Jan-April
Wagener	Early Nov	Dec-April
Warner's King	Late Sept	Nov-Jan
Wellington	Mid Oct	Nov-March
Winston	Oct-early Nov	Jan-April
Worcester Pearmain	Early Sept	Sept-Oct

Pears

Variety	When to pick	Season
Beurré d'Amanlis	Aug	Aug-Sept
Buerré Bedford	Sept	Oct
Beurré Clairgeau	Oct	Nov-Dec
Beurré Diel	Sept	Oct-Dec
Beurré Hardy	Mid Sept	Oct
Beurré Superfin	Sept	Oct
Bristol Cross	Mid Sept	Oct
Catillac	Oct	Dec-April
Cheltenham Cross	End Aug	Sept
Clapp's Favourite	End Aug	Sept
Conference	Late Sept	Oct-Nov
Doyenné d'Eté	July	July-Aug
Doyenné du Comice	Mid Oct	Nov
Dr Jules Guyot	Early Aug	Aug-Sept
Durondeau	Late Sept	Oct-Nov
Easter Beurré	Early Nov	Feb-April
Emile d'Heyst	Late Sept	Oct-Nov
Fertility	Late Sept	Oct
Glou Morceau	Oct	Dec-Jan
Gorham	Early Sept	Sept
Hessle	Sept	Oct
Improved Fertility	Early Sept	Sept-Oct
Jargonelle	Early Aug	Aug
Joséphine de Malines	Late Sept	Dec-Feb
Louise Bonne of Jersey	Late Sept	Oct
Marguerite Marillat	Sept	Sept-Oct
Marie Louise	Late Sept	Oct-Nov
Max Red Bartlett	End Aug	Sept
Merton Pride	Early Sept	Sept-Oct
Nouveau Poiteau	Oct	Nov
Packham's Triumph	Mid Oct	Nov
Passe Crasanne	Early Nov	March-April
Pitmaston Duchess	Late Sept	Oct-Nov
Santa Claus	Late Oct	Dec-Jan
Seckle	Late Sept	Oct-Nov
Souvenir de Congrès	Late Aug	Sept
Thompson's	Early Oct	Oct-Nov
Triomphe de Vienne	Late Aug	Sept
Vicar of Winkfield	Oct	Nov-Jan
Williams' Bon Chrétien	Late Aug	Sept
Winter Nelis	Late Oct	Dec-Jan

1 Harvesting grapes, protected earlier
by cloches, and then allowed to ripen.
2 Pear 'Glou Morceau' ready for
picking. Pears are not left on the tree
too long, otherwise, they go 'sleepy'
when in store, and are useless.

Loganberries grown on nets. Berry fruits are not picked until fully ripe.

woodlice and other pests which may damage the fruit and precautions may have to be taken to prevent mice and rats from entering. Before storing a new season's fruit all shelves and other woodwork and storage trays should be washed down with a solution of copper sulphate to kill disease spores. Exclude daylight except when examining the fruit. Remove any fruits starting to decay. Test pears for ripeness by pressing the neck of the fruit. Condition pears for eating after ripening in store by placing in a warm room at a temperature of approximately 65°F (18°C) for two days.

There are several rots which destroy apples and pears in storage—some of them originate on the fruit while on the tree while others may appear in any store which is allowed to become dirty and · neglected. The most important storage rot in apples is that called gloeosporium rot which often causes dark brown circular saucerlike depressions on the surface of apples just as they become ready to eat. This infection takes place while on the tree and it is important to cut out any cankered shoots and old mummified fruits when pruning, as these places harbour the gloeosporium fungus. Spraying with Captan at three week intervals in autumn also reduces the infection. The fruit should be picked and stored as soon as it is ready. Pick dry if possible but if unavoidably wet, allow to dry off before storing.

Another disease is apple scab, *venturia inaequalis*, well-known to gardeners, but there is often a late infection which appears in the store and in wet seasons a late Captan spray will help. Scab often causes cracking which allows the brown rot fungus, *sclerotinia fructigena*, to enter the scab cracks and quickly rot the apple—it will then spread to the neighbouring ones. Stored apples and pears should therefore always be looked over about three weeks after storing and any diseased ones picked out for burning. Almost all other rotting diseases in the fruit store are due to dirty conditions.

 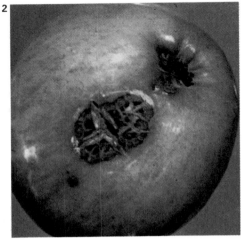

1 Gloeosporium rot on Apples manifests itself in storage by dark depressions.
2 The cracks of Apple Scab allow fungus disease spores to infect the fruit.

Growing vegetables

It is far easier to plan a kitchen garden where the garden is a new one. The gardener who takes over a garden used by previous occupiers may first have to remove shrubs and trees. Not only do trees, shrubs and hedges rob the vegetable garden of plant foods, but they cast shade over the growing plants. Few of the vegetables we grow tolerate shade and the site for the kitchen garden must, therefore, be quite open and unshaded. Brick walls and wood fences cast shade, too, but a wall or fence at the north side is often advantageous in protecting plants from cold north winds. In the past, many kitchen gardens on large estates were laid out in front of a south facing wall and many sites may be made more suitable for vegetable cultivation if wind-breaks are set up to break the force of strong westerly or easterly winds. This is particularly true of gardens in coastal areas and although chestnut or wire mesh fences are worth consideration, living windbreaks such as blackberries are more decorative and useful if trained to a strong trellis.

Provision must be made for paths, a garden shed, the cold frame, a site for compost heaps and possibly for a greenhouse. Even in the large kitchen garden, the number of permanent paths should be the minimum necessary, but sufficiently wide for the barrow to be wheeled comfortably without damage to plants nearby. During the season, temporary paths covered with straw, bracken or peat, allow all crops to be reached with ease. The garden shed may be erected in any out-of-the-way corner provided it is linked to a permanent path so that the gardener does not get wet feet when visiting the shed in winter. The site for the compost heap may be somewhat shaded, but not beneath large, spreading trees. Sufficient room must be left for two heaps because when one is fermenting, another will be built alongside it. There must also be sufficient space left for turning and sifting compost. The gardener who uses animal manure will also leave a few square yards where dung may be stacked. Here shade may be of value in preventing the manure from drying out in summer. Both the cold frame and the greenhouse need a south-facing, open site.

Although most vegetable crops are temporary, rhubarb is generally considered as a permanent kitchen garden crop because the clumps remain in the same soil for around ten years. When allocating a plot for rhubarb, the gardener should bear in mind that although the plants tolerate some shade, crops are better from plants grown at some distance from walls, fences and trees or hedges.

Good cultivation is essential if the best results are to be obtained. The plot should be dug over properly and weeds, both annual and perennial must be kept down.

Vegetables of one plant species do not extract the same quantities of soil chemicals in the ground as do plants of a different species, but the manuring plan and the cropping plan take this into account. After the soil has been well dug and all weeds and weed roots removed, the garden should be divided (on paper or, at any rate mentally) into three plots. These divisions are made so that what is known as crop rotation may be practised. This practice is also aimed at preventing a build up of soil pests in any one part of the garden. It is understandable that if cabbages and their close relatives, for example, are grown for several years in the same piece of ground, the soil will be impoverished (unless the manuring programme is a very generous one) and that pests, which thrive on the roots of the brassica group of plants, are likely to increase. A three year rotation is generally advised and the following plan suggests how this may be carried out.

The kitchen garden is divided into three plots of approximately equal size—A, B and C.

A general view of the kitchen garden in the Royal Horticultural Society's Gardens, Wisley, Surrey. Note how the vegetables are grown in orderly rows and how use is made of frames and cloches.

Cropping plan

First season

Plot A cabbages, brussels sprouts, cauliflower broccoli, turnips

Plot B beans, peas, miscellaneous, small crops

Plot C potatoes, carrots, beetroot, lettuce, onions

Second season The crops shown in Plot C above will be grown on Plot A, crops in Plot A on Plot B and those in Plot B on Plot C

Plot A potatoes etc

Plot B cabbages etc

Plot C beans etc

Third season The position of the crops will be as follows:

Plot A beans etc

Plot B potatoes etc

Plot C cabbages etc

Fourth season In the fourth season, the rotation starts off as in the first year

Until recently the vegetable garden was regularly dressed with animal manures. Those gardeners who are able to obtain farmyard or stable manure (at reasonable prices) are well advised to use them. For all other gardeners, home-made garden compost adequately replaces large quantities of animal manures. Other organic manures such as municipal compost, seaweed, wool shoddy and spent hops are also of great value in maintaining soil fertility and in improving the actual structure of the soil. Manure, compost or other bulky organic materials should not be applied in an unplanned fashion. This is not only because the gardener may have to purchase organic manures but their addition to parts of the garden may lead to poor crops. In the case of parsnips, for instance, the roots are 'fanged' instead of being single, straight and plump, if

1 Using a Mountfield cultivator to prepare the ground.
2 Adding humus to the soil.

the crop is grown in soil which had been recently manured. With other crops, there is generally sufficient food left from a previous manuring.

The following plan suggests how manure, compost or other bulky organics should be applied over three years.

Manuring plan

Plot A cabbages, cauliflowers, brussels sprouts broccoli, kale, savoys, turnips. Possibly inter-cropped with radish and lettuce.
Limed in late autumn, if necessary. Manured or composted during winter digging

Plot B potatoes, followed by broccoli, spring cabbage or leeks.
Not limed. Manured or composted during winter digging

Plot C carrots, parsnips, beetroot, peas, beans summer spinach, onions.
No manure or compost except for pea and bean trenches and for onions. Wood ashes (if available) forked in and a complete fertiliser, such as Growmore, may be applied just before sowings are made

Inter-cropping is referred to in the manuring plan. This practice allows two plants to grow in the place of one. Inter-cropping is of great importance in the small kitchen garden. For good results the soil must be very fertile so that neither of the two crops is starved of food. It is also essential that the rows should run from north to south so that shade does not fall throughout the day from the taller on to the shorter plants. Too much shade of this nature is liable to lead to troubles with pests and diseases. Here is an example of inter-cropping. Rows of peas, which make 3 foot high bine, are sown 3 feet apart, leaving 1 yard between which may be

53

Adding compost while preparing a trench for Beans.

used for radish, spinach or lettuce.

Successional cropping is somewhat similar to inter-cropping because many crops, grown for successional crops, may be cultivated between or alongside vegetables needing more time to reach maturity. The aim of successional cropping is to prevent gluts and shortages. The gardener must be able to assess how many lettuces, peas, summer turnips, radishes etc., the family will require from a single sowing. He sows or sets out plants accordingly and he continues to sow every few weeks, providing he has the space for the sowings. He may start with radish, for example, by sowing three short, close rows under cloches in March. A short, double row is sown outdoors in early April, followed by a sowing between the pea rows in mid-April. Further small sowings are made in May, June and July. By sowing in this manner, there will be a supply of fresh, young radishes from mid-May until October. Lettuce seeds should be sown in small batches between March and August. For successional crops of peas, the gardener should bear in mind that there are early, mid-season and late varieties. All three kinds may be sown at around the same time and the plants will come into bearing successionally. There are also varieties of heading broccoli (cauliflower-broccoli) for cutting during the autumn, late winter, spring and early summer. With potatoes, there are kinds which bulk up for lifting in June and July; others mature more slowly for late summer use. Main-crop potatoes are not dug and stored until the autumn.

Catch-cropping, like inter-cropping, is aimed at using every available square inch of the garden. It means no more than making use of any vacant plot for a quick-growing vegetable. Radishes may be sown in April on the site reserved for outdoor tomatoes. The radish crop will have been pulled for use before the tomatoes are set out. The soil banked on either side of leek or celery trenches may be cropped with radish or lettuce.

Even the most experienced gardeners quite often fail to regulate the supply of vegetables throughout the year. In most cases, the weather is to blame. A warm June, for instance, may hasten the summer and autumn cabbage crops but lead to disaster among the lettuces which bolt at once after forming hearts. A severe winter may cripple broccoli and spring cabbages. So very often, too, due to the vagaries of the weather, there are many fine lettuce and radish for use when the family is away on holiday. Arrangements should be made for these crops to be harvested and shared by neighbours while the family is away. Unless friends, relations or neighbours help in this way, the gardener is likely to return from holiday to find his bean plants covered with a useless crop of old, stringy pods.

Planning starts in January when the seed catalogues are studied and orders placed for seeds and seed potatoes. Variety is of great importance and the good gardener is always able to harvest something fresh at any time of the year. During the winter, home-grown produce generally consists of cabbage and allied greens together with fresh or stored roots. The owner of a large kitchen garden should consider buying a deep freeze cabinet in which surplus summer vegetables and soft fruits may be stored for winter use so that the diet is more varied. The forcing of such crops as seakale, chicory and endive is another way of preventing monotony in winter fare.

No kitchen garden is complete, nor can the diet be so varied, without the use of at least one form of glass (or possibly plastic) protection. These are frames, cloches or greenhouse. For the use of cloches see chapter 5.

The garden frame Frames make use of trapped sun heat and also protect plants by four sides and removable top or light. Sowings may be made earlier in the cold frame than in the open. During

1 Raking to break down the lumps.
2 Preparing a drill before planting.
3 Planting Cabbages in rows.

4 Planting Potatoes in a prepared drill, using a garden line.
5 Covering Potatoes after planting.

6 Catch-cropping: sowing Lettuces on the soil from a Celery trench.

the summer, melons and cucumbers may be grown in the cold frame. The winter use of the cold frame is to house plants of lettuce, cabbage, cauliflower and onion.

Many different models are available. Some have a brick or concrete base with sides of glass; others have brick, concrete or wooden sides. The frame light may be hinged or sliding and the

Well-grown plants in a kitchen garden, the Peas protected by netting.

framework may be wood or metal. Many practical gardeners construct their own garden frames and one may be easily and cheaply made. A large frame is far better than a small one, not only because there is more space for crops, but also because the atmosphere of the small frame is quickly influenced by outside temperatures. It is in the small frame that lettuce and cauliflower plants freeze in severe winter weather or melon plants wilt because of extremely high temperatures in August.

A seed bed may be prepared in the cold frame in early March and sowings of lettuce, summer cabbage, Brussels sprouts, leeks and onions made as soon as weather conditions seem favourable to quick germination. Plants of half hardy vegetables such as dwarf and runner beans, tomatoes, ridge cucumbers, melons, pumpkin and marrow may also be raised in the cold frame. The seeds should not, however, be sown until early April in the case of tomatoes and later that month for the others. In the case of half hardy vegetables, the seeds should not be sown in the bed of the frame but in peat pots sunk in the bed. Particular attention must be paid to watering and ventilation as well as to

1 Frames, if properly utilised, can make the kitchen garden much more productive.
2 Ventilating the frame is necessary in hot weather.
3 Sweet Corn plants, started in a frame; the light has now been removed.
4 Sowing seeds of Tomatoes in pots.
5 Frame-grown Tomatoes.
6 Sowing Runner Beans in pots in the greenhouse in spring.

protection at night if frosts may occur.

Good summer frame crops are self blanching celery, tomatoes, melons and cucumbers. Tomato and celery plants may be set out in mid May and the light removed in June. Melon and cucumber plants are set out in early June and the light is not removed.

Tomatoes ripening under glass.

Season of use of most vegetables

Month	Fresh from the garden	Fresh from under glass	From store	Blanched	Dried
January and February	Brussels sprouts cabbage, celery coleworts Hamburgh parsley kale, leeks parsnips salsify spinach, tree onions	mustard cress	potatoes artichokes carrots garlic onions pumpkin shallots winter radish	chicory endive seakale	peas haricot beans
March	Brussels tops cabbage, kale leeks, spinach turnip tops tree onions Welsh onions for salads, leeks	lettuce mustard cress	potatoes carrots garlic onions	chicory	peas haricot beans
April	cauliflower- broccoli, leeks kale, spinach sprouting broccoli turnip tops Welsh onions	lettuce mustard cress radish rhubarb	potatoes garlic onions	chicory	peas haricot beans
May	asparagus cauliflower- broccoli, kale spinach, rhubarb spring greens spring cabbages sprouting broccoli turnip tops Welsh onions	lettuce radish rhubarb	potatoes garlic		
June	asparagus potatoes, peas broad beans, lettuce cabbage, rhubarb spring onions	lettuce	potatoes		

Season of use of most vegetables

Month	Fresh from the garden	Fresh from under glass	From store	Blanched	Dried
July	beetroot, cabbage broad beans, peas carrots, dwarf beans courgettes globe artichokes kohlrabi, potatoes spinach, spring onions radish, turnips vegetable marrow	tomatoes			
August	as for July plus: cucumbers, calabrese self blanching celery runner beans, melons sweet corn, tomatoes	tomatoes cucumbers melons aubergines sweet peppers	garlic		
September	as for August except: dwarf beans, broad beans, globe artichokes but with cauliflowers	as for August	garlic		
October	beetroot, cabbage, cauliflower, cauliflower-broccoli, celery celeriac, kohlrabi turnips, swedes, winter radish	tomatoes lettuce	potatoes, onions carrots garlic tomatoes	endive chicory	
November and December	cabbage cauliflower-broccoli celery, celeriac parsnips, salsify Brussels sprouts spinach artichokes Hamburgh parsley	lettuce mustard and cress corn salad	artichokes garlic pumpkin potatoes swedes onions carrots shallots	endive chicory seakale	peas haricot beans

Note: Savoys are included as cabbages during the winter months

1 Harvesting Onions. The tops were bent over earlier and have now dried. The bulbs have been lifted and are now being collected for final drying off in the greenhouse before they are stored for winter use.
2 Harvesting Potatoes. The plants were grown under black polythene sheeting which acts as a mulch, keeping down weeds and helping to retain soil moisture.

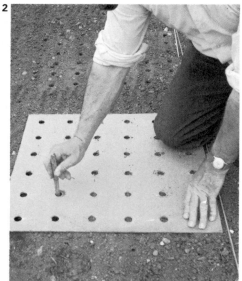

The greenhouse As far as vegetables are concerned, the garden frame and cloches are considered to be more useful than the greenhouse. As with cold frames, the smaller the unheated greenhouse, the quicker the temperature rises and falls. Adequate ventilation must be given and a thermometer is a most useful instrument.

In a slightly heated greenhouse, the gardener may grow out of season crops. Having tomatoes in June and cucumbers in July, when shop prices may be high, is very much worth while. In the north, the artificial heat will allow the gardener to raise his own tomato, cucumber, sweet corn and melon plants. The experienced gardener will also grow a winter crop of lettuce. Great skill is necessary in the production of out of season vegetables and only experience can teach the gardener, provided he accepts the guidance offered him in a book such as this.

1 Setting out Celery plants in a trench, using a planting stick to keep the plants in straight rows.
2 A board, with holes drilled at 4-inches apart, is a useful accessory when sowing seeds of root crops.
3 Sowing Peas in staggered rows.

Hotbeds When fresh farmyard manure is plentiful, light frames may be set on heaps of fermenting manure to produce conditions similar to a heated greenhouse.

Vegetables under cloches

Cloches are designed to give protection and this feature can be made use of in several ways. During wet or cold weather the soil can be covered with cloches and kept dry and warm. This enables the gardener to sow or plant much earlier than usual. Protection from cold winds and low temperatures encourages earlier and quicker growth and many plants can be started several weeks earlier than normally. In the colder northern counties and elsewhere many valuable winter crops can be brought through severe conditions successfully. Cloches stood securely on edge or wrapped around tender, larger plants, afford protection from cold prevailing winds and will promote healthier growth.

Two or three cloches placed together with their ends sealed with glass, make ideal propagators or miniature frames. If the larger type of cloche is used a number of seedlings can be raised in a comparatively small area.

Cloches protect plants from bird

Lettuces grown under cloches can be planted in two or three staggered rows. Spacing between the rows and the plants needs to be reasonably accurate.

damage. Many seedlings are attacked by birds, especially pigeons, in town gardens. Seedlings raised under cloches are given complete protection.

Planning and Preparation Cloche cultivation is an intensive form of gardening and from a small piece of ground a wide variety of produce can be gathered. Cloches are used in continuous rows or strips, which must be sealed at the ends by a sheet of glass, retained in position by a piece of cane or strong wire. The number of rows or strips which are used will depend on the amount of ground available.

One of the best ways to use cloches is to lay down a double row on a 6 foot wide strip of ground with a 4–6 inch gap between the two cloche rows. This 6 foot wide strip will also include a 2 foot wide path. The rest of the cloche garden is marked out into several of these 6 foot wide strips. If the plot is laid out in this way, the cloches will not have to be moved far when they are transferred from one crop to another.

The basic system of cropping is as follows: a double row is planted or sown and covered with cloches. Later on the vacant double strip near them and separated by the 2 foot wide path is sown or planted. The cloches from the first double strip are moved over to cover this newly cropped strip, leaving the de-cloched crop to mature in the open. As soon as this crop has been cleared, the ground is prepared and another crop sown or planted. In due course, the cloches on the second strip are moved back on to the first strip and the crop just de-cloched is either gathered or

allowed to mature in the open. This to and fro movement keeps the cloches continually in use. It is possible to devise more ambitious cropping schemes which require more strips and rows of

Lettuces are an ideal crop for cultivation under cloches. The protection afforded ensures an early, more succulent crop protected from birds. A cultivar such as 'Mayfair' is good for early cropping.

cloches.

The intensiveness of cropping can be increased still further if inter-cropping is practised. This means the cultivation of a quick maturing crop in the same strip as a slower growing main crop. The former is gathered several weeks before the latter is ready. An example of this is the cultivation of a centre row of sweet peas under a rown of cloches, with a row of lettuce on either side of the peas. The lettuces grow rapidly and will be cleared before the sweet peas become tall.

Crop selection Intensive gardening such as this cannot be successful unless the crops and their varieties are selected with some care. Most of the cloche crops can be divided into these three sections:
(a) Hardy plants which crop in early spring. Sowings are made under cloches in late autumn and winter and are kept covered until early April.
(b) Half-hardy plants which are covered during April and May.
(c) Tender plants which require cloche coverage during the summer.

Soil preparation Soil moisture must be conserved under cloches as the ground is covered for long periods and protection from rain and the higher temperatures produced under the cloches can cause rapid drying out. To combat this, as much humus material as possible is worked into the ground to act as a sponge which retains moisture for long periods.

The humus can take the form of well-rotted manure worked in at the rate of a barrowload to 8 yards of strip; horticultural peat at a barrowload to 5 yards a strip or composted vegetable waste at a barrowload to 6 yards of strip. The strips are marked out with a line and dug over as deeply as possible to ensure good drainage. As the strip is prepared the humus material is worked into the bottom of each short trench. Where soils are light, some additional peat should be worked into the top 3–4 inches. This is also done when a small cloche seed bed is prepared.

Each year, at a convenient time in the planning of a new rotation system, the 2 foot wide path should be dug over and used as part of a growing strip. In this way, over the years, a very rich area of cloche ground is maintained.

Growing vegetables A week before sowing or planting takes place a well-balanced or general fertiliser is given at 3 oz per square yard. This is raked in thoroughly and the raking action will also break the soil down ready for sowing or planting. If cloches are placed over the prepared strips a week before sowing or planting takes place, the ground will be warmed slightly and will be maintained in a suitable condition despite bad weather.

Beetroot For early supplies, a late February sowing is made in the south. For general sowings March is a suitable month. Small or large cloches are used depending on the number of rows required. Sow a single row under small cloches, three rows under larger ones, spacing these 6 inches apart. All seed is sown as thinly as possible, about 1 inch deep. Early thinning is necessary when seedlings can be handled easily. A later thinning is advised when roots the size of a golf ball are lifted. These are excellent for salads. Plants left in the rows are allowed to mature. 'Detroit Selected' and 'Crimson Ball' are suitable.

Broad beans Seed is sown in mid November in the north and late January in the south. Tall cloches or additional height provided by special strong wire adaptors is necessary in late spring for frost protection to tall plants. Sow a double row in a 3 inch deep, flat bottom drill which is 8 inches wide. Space the seeds 8 inches apart in staggered fashion. Two suitable varieties are 'Aquadulce' and 'Early Long Pod'.

Dwarf Beans Three sowings can be made: mid March in the south, early April in the north and, for a late crop to be picked approximately in October, a July sowing can be made. For all sowings the variety 'Lightning' is ideal. Seed is sown under the larger cloches in a double row in a flat 6 inch wide trench, 2 inches deep. Stagger seeds 8 inches apart. If drying beans are required, haricots should be sown in mid April in all districts as above. A good variety to use is 'Comtesse du Chambourd'.

Runner Beans In the south seed is sown in mid March and in late April in the north. Large barn cloches are used making a double row sowing with the rows 9 inches apart. Seeds are placed 2 inches deep and 8–10 inches apart. As the plants are staked individually later on, the seeds are not staggered, but placed opposite each other. 'Streamline' and 'Kelvedon Wonder' are extremely reliable.

Brussel Sprouts Cloches are used solely as seed raisers to give plants a long growing period after and early start. Seed is sown thinly in shallow drills under one or more cloches. Young plants are pricked out later into another seed bed and finally planted 2½ feet apart each way in their permanent quarters. In the south a sowing can be made in late January using varieties such as 'Cambridge No. 1' for early pickings and 'Cambridge No. 5' for late crops. As soon as conditions allow in the north a sowing can be made in February using 'Cambridge No. 1' or 'The Wroxton'.

Carrots Five sowings are made according to district. In the south early January will provide the first pickings if the variety 'Primo' is used. The earliest possible sowing date in the north is mid to late February with a variety such as 'Early Nantes'. Gardeners in the south can make another sowing in February for a prolonged supply of the early 'Primo'. For a late November supply of carrots in the north, an August sowing of 'Primo' is advised. The seedlings must be cloched in September before first frosts threaten. Late crops for southern gardeners are obtained if a September to October sowing is made using the varieties 'Early Nantes' or 'Primo'. Large cloches should be used, and four or five rows can be accommodated. Thin sowing is necessary in ¼ inch deep drills spaced 4–5 inches apart.

Cauliflowers Three sowings can be made, using a cloche or two as a seed raiser. Early September for the north and late September for the south are the first sowing dates for early crops. Large cloches should be used so that three drills can be made. Sow thinly and thin later to 2 inches apart. Plant out finally in March and April 2 feet apart each way. If very large cloches are available, some plants can be covered to maturity. A suitable variety for these sowings is 'All The Year Round'. In the south a further sowing can be made in January and late in February for northern

districts. In both instances plants are raised under a few cloches and finally planted out in outdoor beds. The same variety can be used.

Cucumbers Frame and ridge types can be used. The former is hardier and cloche protection is necessary during early stages of growth only. Plants can be purchased and set out under cloches in late April or seed can be raised under a cloche in early April in the south and late April or early May in the north. Whichever method is adopted, plants are finally planted out 3 feet apart in a single row. For each plant a special site should be prepared, taking out a hole 1 foot square and half filling it with old manure or composted vegetable waste. The remainder of the hole should be filled up with good soil, mixed with a little horticultural peat.

Plants are trained in a special way. When the fourth true leaf has formed, the growing point of the plant is removed. Several lateral growths should form and the two strongest are selected; the others removed. These two are trained to run along the direction of the cloche row, one on either side of the plant. When these growths have produced six leaves, they are stopped. Side growths should form on the laterals and it is on these that the fruit is carried. All side growths are stopped at the third leaf beyond a fruit. Growths not bearing fruit are stopped at the sixth leaf.

All male flowers must be removed regularly from plants, otherwise fruits will be bitter and malformed. This applies only to the frame type of cucumber. Plenty of water is necessary and as soon as the first fruits have formed, weak liquid feeds or dry fertiliser should be given. Some light shading of the glass may be advisable in very warm, bright weather. Suitable varieties to use are 'Conqueror', 'Improved Telegraph', and 'Butcher's Disease Resisting' which

1 Young cucumbers grown under cloches require to be shaded from strong sunlight.
2 Sweet peas benefiting from cloche protection, with a catch crop of lettuce.

1 Radish, the quick maturing 'French Breakfast'. 2 Marrows can be encouraged to set fruit early with cloche protection.

early September to protect from early frosts. The plants must be blanched or whitened. This is easily done if a flat object such as an inverted plate or saucer is placed over the centre of each plant. In about six weeks the leaves will have blanched sufficiently. The best variety is 'Round-leaved Batavian'.

Lettuce Late September is the sowing time in all districts for lettuce which will be ready for cutting from approximately March to May. Large barn cloches are used to accommodate three rows of seeds. Sow thinly and thin in November to 10 inches apart. Cloches remain over until April or late May in colder districts. Suitable varieties are 'Attraction' and 'May King'.

In late January a further sowing can be made in southern counties. These lettuce should be ready for cutting in June. Similar growing techniques are required except that the original sowing must be even thinner to minimise thinning or transplanting checks. 'May King' and 'Perpetual' are good varieties.

Northern gardeners should make a sowing in late March. When large enough to handle thin plants to 1 foot apart. Cloches can be removed in early June when frost danger has passed. 'Trocadero Improved', 'Wonderful' and 'Buttercrunch' are ideal varieties.

For a late November supply of lettuce in the north, a sowing can be made in late July. Thin plants to at least 1 foot

are frame types, and 'Best of All Ridge', 'Greenline' and 'Long Green' which are ridge cucumbers.

Endive This is a useful crop which replaces lettuce in districts where lettuce cultivation is not very successful. In the south an early June sowing is ideal and later that month in northern gardens. Two rows are sown thinly under large barn cloches, spacing the rows 1 foot apart and sowing the seed ½ inch deep. Seedlings are thinned eventually to 1 foot apart. The crop is covered in

apart to allow plenty of air to circulate round plants in the dull months. Put cloches over the plants in early September. 'May King', 'Market Favourite' and 'Attraction' can be recommended.

The most suitable time to sow cos lettuce in all districts is March. Cover immediately with cloches which are removed in early June. Two rows can be sown under a large barn cloche. Seedlings must be thinned to 1 foot apart. A good variety to sow is 'Giant White'.

Marrow Sow in late April in the north

and late March in the south. Culture is similar to that required for cucumbers except that the compact bush types are the best to grow. These require no stopping or training. To ensure a good set of fruit, hand pollination is advisable. The cloches are kept over the plants until early June. Suitable varieties are 'Tender and True', 'Green or White Bush' and 'Courgette'.

Peas For first sowings in the north, early October is the best month and southern sowings are carried out in November. The next sowing in the south is January and both north and south can sow again in March.

Sow in 8 inches wide flat drills, 2 inches deep. The seed is scattered in staggered formation 2–3 inches apart each way in three rows. The cloches remain over the plants from early sowings until the foliage is practically touching the roof glass. The peas can be decloched in early April when seed is sown in March. Early training with small twigs or brushwood is essential for good growth. Plenty of water is required once the plants are well established from the spring onwards. Suitable varieties are 'Meteor' for the October or November sowings, 'Kelvedon Wonder' for January sowings and 'Laxton's Superb' for the March sowings.

Radish This crop (like the lettuce and early carrots), is an ideal catch crop or intercrop. Out of season sowings are more valuable for cloche work and in the south sowings are made in late September and frequently from then onwards until late March. For northern

gardeners, September and October are suitable months for late work and the end of February until late April for the early spring. Seed is sown thinly in shallow drills when used as a catch crop or broadcast under one or two cloches. The smaller cloches are particularly suitable for the latter purpose. Suitable varieties are 'French Breakfast' and 'Scarlet Globe'.

Sweet Corn This is one crop in particular which is grown more easily in this country with the aid of cloches. In the north a sowing can be made in early May, and in the south in the second or

third week in April. Seed is sown *in situ* or where the plants are to grow to maturity. Sow seed 10 inches apart in double rows spaced 1 foot apart. Two seeds per station are sown, removing the weakest seedling later on. This crop should not be transplanted. When the foliage reaches the roof the crop can be decloched. Plenty of water is essential during hot, dry weather. There is no need to remove sidegrowths. A little soil should be drawn up on either side

Cloches in pairs stood on end to protect young tomato plants.

of the rows when the plants are about 3 feet high. This helps to anchor them and is an essential part of their culture in exposed districts. The cobs are ripe when the grain inside the cobs exudes a milky fluid as they are squeezed with the finger nails. Suitable varieties are 'Fogwill's Extra Early', 'Golden Bantam' and 'Canada Crop'.

Tomatoes Outdoor tomatoes are usually a rather chancy crop in this country as a long spell of good weather is needed to get the bulk of the fruit ripened before frosts cut the plants down. Cloches have an invaluable part to play in the successful culture of this plant. They can either give the plants vital early protection so that they become established quickly or they can provide continuous protection which will produce crops nearly as early as glasshouse ones. Northern gardeners will welcome this type of protection in districts which are much colder.

The site for the crop should be prepared thoroughly by deep cultivation. Separate positions can be prepared for each plant as for cucumbers and marrows. A general fertiliser is applied a few days before planting at 3 oz per square yard. The plants are best purchased from a reliable source. Good plants are short jointed and deep green in colour. The plants should be set out 2 feet apart in the row, with 3 feet

1 A well shaped truss of tomatoes ripening in early summer. The plants were given cloche protection after planting out.
2 A small vegetable garden which has been developed to its fullest.

between each row.

Two shapes of tomato plant can be grown, the cordon and the bush. Where it is intended to grow entirely under cloches, the bush type is ideal. As soon as the plants have been set out they should be staked and tied securely. All sideshoots must be removed from cordon plants as soon as they are noticed. In early June, it will be safe enough in all districts to remove the cloches entirely except where it is intended to grow to maturity under them. Plenty of water must be given, especially when the first flower trusses have set. Dry or weak liquid feeds will be required to encourage heavy trusses of fruit.

When cordon plants have produced four trusses, they should be stopped. This is done by removing the centre or growing point of the plants. Bush tomatoes require no stopping or side-shooting. Several varieties can be grown out of doors. Of the cordons, 'Outdoor Girl' and 'Essex Wonder' are excellent. There are several very good bush varieties. These include 'Amateur Improved', 'Atom' and 'Dwarf Cloche'.

A cropping plan For one row of barn cloches used on the two strip system.

Strip 1		Strip 2	
October-April		**April-May**	
Lettuce	1 row	Dwarf Beans	
Radish	1 row		
Peas	centre row	**October-April**	
		Lettuce	1 row
June-September		Radish	1 row
Cucumber		Peas	centre row

If in January you study seed catalogues and make your selections, your summer reward can be vegetables in abundance. New introductions, including some suitable for the deep-freeze, can make your garden more productive.